4

Oh, Yeah? Proof It!

Frank Schaffer
An imprint of Carson-Dellosa Publishing LLC
Greensboro, North Carolina

Frank Schaffer Publications®
An imprint of Carson-Dellosa Publishing LLC
P.O. Box 35665
Greensboro, NC 27425 USA

 ISBN 0-7682-3654-1

1 2 3 4 5 6 7 8 9 10 GLO 15 14 13 12 11 10

Table of Contents

Letter from the Publisher

Teachers, Family Members, and Other Caregivers:

Proofreading is an essential skill when writing and evaluating the writing of others. As students grow more skilled in proofreading, they hone their ability to quickly spot and correct their own errors, as well as the errors of classmates. This heightens their awareness of grammar and other skills necessary to write well.

Oh, Yeah? Proof It! is designed with a scaffolded approach. Proofreading skills are initially isolated. Then, they are integrated into the writing tasks with skills already addressed. Ultimately, students are called upon to exercise all the proofreading skills they have learned throughout the book. Such scaffolding allows students to experience a mastery and confidence with specific skills before moving ahead to tackle others. This approach ultimately prepares them for the wrap-up activities that appear at the end of the book, as well as proofreading they will engage in throughout their lives.

Sincerely,
Frank Schaffer Publications

Proofreading Marks

This is how you show a change from a capital letter to a lowercase letter. Doctor	Use this mark to add underlining. Ramona Quimby, Age 8
This is how you show a change from a lowercase letter to a capital letter. chicago	Use this mark to take away underlining. Ramona Quimby, Age 8
Use this mark to add a period if it is missing. Tues.	Use this mark to add an apostrophe. dont
Use this mark to add an end mark. This is my dog. Is this my dog? What a dog!	Use this mark to take away an apostrophe. don't'
This is how you take out an end mark and add a new end mark. Is this my dog.?	Use this mark to take away a word or a letter. I don't not like Nobody never goes there.
Use this mark to add a comma. Houston, Texas	This is how to take away one word or letter and add another. their They left there bats in the gym.
Use this mark to add a quotation mark. Don said, "Let's go home."	Use this mark to show a new paragraph. ¶
This is how you move a quotation mark to a new location. "Don said, "Let's go home."	

BOBCAT NEWS

NEWS

Read the article. The writer has made some mistakes with capital letters. Use proofreading marks to correct the mistakes.

REMEMBER!

- Every sentence must begin with a capital letter.
  We live near the park.
- A common noun does not begin with a capital letter and names a person, place, or thing.
  Common Nouns: child, town, pet
- A proper noun begins with a capital letter and names a specific person, place, or thing.
  Proper Nouns: Jan, Seattle, Muffy
- This is how you show a change from a capital letter to a lowercase letter.
  Child
- This is how you show a change from a lowercase letter to a capital letter.
  seattle

Car Wash

by Sue Mofta

The car wash at nearby jefferson high school was a great success. It gave us many Ideas for our own school car Wash next Year. My Sister, anya, was in charge of the event.

many hours of planning went into the event. students put up posters in Stores across the city. They handed out coupons at a local Floral shop named flowers are us. students also found a bakery, jake's cakes, to give refreshments for the workers.

to prepare, Students set up soap, Buckets, hoses, Gloves, and rags. they used a special kind of soap that is not bad for the Environment. drivers entered through the South entrance of the parking lot. three Students worked on each Car to wash, rinse, and dry It.

Almost sixty Cars were washed. students worked in shifts of two Hours. there were plenty of students to help. many Family members and Teachers helped.

At the end of the Day, students were tired, and the Parking Lot at the High School was very soapy! students cleaned up everything and looked forward to Events that would be possible because of Money from the car wash.

A. *Correctly rewrite the article.*

B. *Write an article of your own on a separate piece of paper.*

- [ ] Include an article title and your name.
- [ ] Tell something interesting about a city you have visited—or would like to visit.
- [ ] Include names of people in the article.
- [ ] Make sure to begin all sentences with a capital letter.
- [ ] Make sure to begin all common nouns with a lowercase letter.
- [ ] Make sure to begin all proper nouns with a capital letter.

Student Stories

Read the student's story. The writer has made some mistakes with capital letters. Use proofreading marks to correct the mistakes.

Remember!

- The word *I* is always capitalized.
  My neighbor and I walk to school.
- When using the name of a family member, such as *Mom* or *Dad,* as a name or in direct address, begin the word with a capital letter.
  He asked his mom if he could stay longer.
  He asked, "Mom, may I stay longer?"
  I'd like to wish you a very happy birthday, Mom.
- Remember the rules you have learned about capital letters.
- Remember the marks for capital and lowercase letters. Turn to page 5 if you need to review the marks.

To Play or Not to Play?

by Tim Strang

Hakeem preferred to spend more time playing the Piano than doing almost anything else. the thought of playing in front of others made him shake and quake. His Dad would often ask, "hakeem, wouldn't you like to play piano at school?"

Hakeem would always give the same answer. "You know, dad, that i am too scared to play in front of the school. What if i make a mistake?"

At school the following week, hakeem's Sister walked over. "We have a chance to win new computers for the School. There's a music competition. I told grandpa just last week that i think you are one of the best piano Players i have ever heard. Will You do it?"

Hakeem just hung his head and walked away. Then, ms. chang stopped Him in the hall. she'd heard about how well he played. she told him, "Our school computers have gotten really old. Please, will You play in the competition?"

Hakeem's heart raced. But He knew what He had to do. He agreed to help his School.

A. *Correctly rewrite the article.*

B. *Use proofreading marks to correct the mistakes with capitals in the sentences below.*

1. Did You know that i asked my Mom for a new pair of skates?

2. he said, "Please help me, grandma."

3. She gave the report to her Teacher, mr. Ling.

4. My Dad and i will go to dinner at the Restaurant.

Classifieds

Read the ad. The writer has made some mistakes with capital letters. Use proofreading marks to correct the mistakes.

Remember!

- Use a capital letter to begin names of days of the week, months of the year, and holidays.

  We will leave for vacation on Tuesday, November 20.

  We'll come back home the day after Labor Day.

- Remember the marks for capital and lowercase letters. Turn to page 5 if you need to review the marks.

Giant Sale at Skate Time

You won't believe the deals you'll find at skate time! be sure to cut out the coupon at the bottom of the page. You can use it only on Friday, may 1.

Sale Dates

thursday, april 30–wednesday, may 5

We won't have another sale until the Day after thanksgiving, so get the good deals now!

Big, Big Specials

On friday, all helmets will be half price.

all skates will be half price on saturday.

you can buy all skate Books for half price on monday.

Use this coupon on friday, may 1.

This coupon is good on one Day only. bring it in to receive $1.00 off of any purchase.

Correctly rewrite the ad.

Giant Sale at Skate Time

Letters to the Editor

Read the letter to the editor. The writer has made some mistakes with capital letters. Use proofreading marks to correct the mistakes.

Remember!

- Use a capital letter to begin the name of a city, state, country, or street.
- State abbreviations are always two capital letters.
  I live at 345 Smith Street in Oshkosh, Wisconsin.

  Tam Ruiz
451 King Lane
Oshkosh, WI
- Use a capital letter to begin a proper adjective.
  Italian Polish Swedish

Paris

Dear Ms. Jula:

We have been studying many cultures. Our teacher has asked us to write letters to the editor to explain what we learned about other Countries. My cousin and my aunt and uncle are french. They live in paris, france. My dad and I went to visit them last year.

The plane ride was almost ten hours long! While we were on the plane, small screens showed a Map. A little airplane on the Map showed where we were. I could see the locations of many of the Countries we have studied. I saw england, italy, france, and many other Countries.

In paris, we visited the eiffel tower and went to Museums, Palaces, and Gardens. Many people walk and take the metro in paris. The metro is sort of like the subway in new york. Most of the cars on the Street are very small, and there are not very many places to park.

My dad has friends who are irish and italian. We wanted to visit ireland and italy on our trip, but we didn't have enough time. My report and other students' reports will be posted in the hall near the fourth grade classrooms. We hope students will come by to read the reports and see the pictures.

Sincerely,

Nia Lang

Nia Lang

A. *Correctly rewrite the letter to the editor.*

B. *Circle the address that is correctly capitalized. Then, use proofreading marks to correct the addresses that are not correct.*

234 jones Road
Houston, Tx

599 Oak Lane
New Orleans, LA

922 Rula Avenue
San Diego, ca

710 silas Street
Philadelphia, PA

Summer Blog Post

Read the blog post. The writer has made some mistakes with capital letters. Use proofreading marks to correct the mistakes.

Remember!

- Use a capital letter to begin all words in the greeting of a letter.

  Dear Ms. Martinez:

  To My Good Friend,

- Use a capital letter to begin only the first word in the closing of letter.

  Your good friend,

  Your grandson,

- Remember the marks for capital and lowercase letters. Turn to page 5 if you need to review the marks.

Damaged Backpacks

To My school friends,

One of the teachers and I ordered backpacks for members of the Camp scouts of America at our school. The backpacks arrived. They were all damaged. They had broken zippers, broken clips, and tears.

I tried to call the company, but no one would help on the phone. I finally sent a letter to the company owner. I explained that we had decided to order from the company because the Society for the prevention of cruelty to Animals had ordered from the same Web site. The people there said the items they received were in excellent condition.

I explained that we liked the look and size of the backpacks. But I also explained all the problems. I told them we'd planned to order from the Company again next year, but we needed these backpacks replaced. Guess what? They sent us new ones! If anyone from the Franklin elementary School drama Club or another club wants to order from the company, I'll give you the information.

Your Friend,

Nanette Lapour

Write a short blog post to a friend or your class. Explain how you solved a problem. Include a greeting and a closing.

RESOURCES

Read the ad. The writer has made some mistakes with capital letters. Use proofreading marks to correct the mistakes.

REMEMBER!

- Use a capital letter to begin the first word in the title of a song, poem, book, or play.
- Use a capital letter to begin important words in the title of a song, poem, book, or play.
- Do not use capital letters for these unimportant words in a title: a, an, at, the, in, of—unless the word is the first word of the title.

  Treasure Island

  The Cricket in Times Square
- Use a capital letter for the first word in a quotation.

  My brother said, "Let's get ready for the party."
- Remember the marks for capital and lowercase letters. Turn to page 5 if you need to review the marks.

Resources for Reports

At the beginning of the school year, teachers post a list of good resources for your research reports in the school newspaper. The list for fourth grade is posted here. Additions to the list will be made later. Mr. Lyle says, "our resources this year are very strong." Ms. Halda says, "please speak to one of your own teachers if you have questions about these resources."

Resource List

Books

Biography Of Frederick Douglass

the beginning of America

Susan B. Anthony And Women's rights

Songs

"the country's Banner"

"stars And stripes forever"

"trying To Begin Our lives In A new Place"

Plays

an Author's world

the Wizard Of oz

A Bull In A China Shop

Poems

"afternoon On a Hill"

"Stopping By Woods on A Snowy evening"

"Looking up At The snowy peaks"

Correctly rewrite the titles. Then, add two new titles to each list. You may write the titles of any books, plays, songs, and poems you know.

Resource List

Books

____

____

____

____

____

Songs

____

____

____

____

____

Plays

____

____

____

____

____

Poems

____

____

____

____

____

BOOK REVIEW

Read the book review.
The writer has made some mistakes with capital letters.
Use proofreading marks to correct the mistakes.

REMEMBER!

- Remember what you have learned about capitalization.
- Remember the marks for capital and lowercase letters. Turn to page 5 if you need to review the marks.

A Wrinkle in Time

In this Book, a Sister and Brother travel through time and space. they know they must save their Father. It was nice that the Author let the Sister and Brother solve the problems in the book.

This is a strong example of science fiction. it catches the Reader's interest from the first moment, and it is interesting from beginning to end. I won't give away the meaning of the title of the Book, but i would urge everyone to read it to figure out what the title means.

I would strongly recommend A wrinkle in time. It is one of the finest books I have ever read. This book was written by madeleine L'Engle. she writes descriptions that make you feel as though you are traveling through time right along with the characters.

The plot in this Book is strong. The action draws in the reader, and then the action builds and builds. Without a doubt, i recommend this book.

A. *Correctly rewrite the book review.*

B. *Circle the choice that shows correct capitalization.*

1. a. Dr. mitchell and Mr. Ganesh
   b. Dr. Mitchell and Mr. Ganesh
   c. dr. mitchell and Mr. Ganesh

2. a. He asked, "Dad, could we go to see a movie?"
   b. He asked, "dad, could we go to see a movie?"
   c. he asked, "dad, could we go to see a movie?"

3. a. French and Russian cultures
   b. french and Russian cultures
   c. French and russian cultures

4. a. Girl scouts of America
   b. Girl Scouts of America
   c. Girl Scouts of america

5. a.

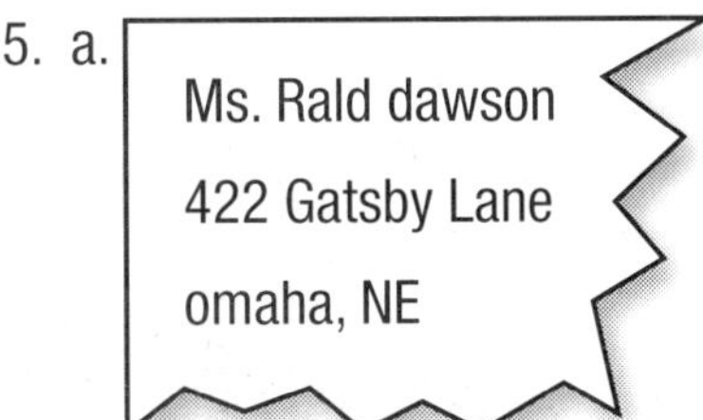

b.

Ms. Rald Dawson
422 Gatsby Lane
Omaha, NE

c.

Ms. Rald Dawson
422 Gatsby Lane
Omaha, ne

IMPORTANT DATES

Read the event list. The writer has made some mistakes with abbreviations. Use proofreading marks to correct the mistakes.

REMEMBER!

- An abbreviation is a shortened form of a word. Almost all abbreviations begin with a capital letter and end with a period.
  Thurs. Fri. Jan. Feb.
  Mr. Ms. Dr.
  Ln. Dr. Rd. Ave.
- Use this mark to add a period if it is missing.
  Tues.
- Use this mark to take away a period that does not belong.
  TX.
- Remember the marks for capital and lowercase letters.

Important Fall Events

- Drama Club will meet on wed after school every week. See mr Bhatt for more information.
- Science Club will meet on thurs before school every week. The advisor is dr Johnston.
- Meetings to prepare for the winter fundraiser will be held on the last mon in aug and the first mon in sept this fall. Ms Wu is in charge.
- The orchestra will meet before school on tues through fri in the band room. Talk to ms Lang if you have questions.
- Chorus members will meet after school on wed and thurs each week. For more information, see mr Abraham.
- Planning for the fall fair will be held on each mon during the month of oct at school. The room number for the meetings will be posted later.
- We will post more fall information in upcoming issues. We will post information for the spring in the jan issue of the newspaper. Send an e-mail to Ms Sloan if you have items to be included.

A. *Write a list of your classes or activities for three months. Include at least six activities on the list. Abbreviate all months and days of the week. Include abbreviations for at least five days of the week and three months.*

B. *Write the names of five teachers you have now or have had in the past. Write the name of a doctor whose name you have seen or heard. Use abbreviations for the people's titles.*

C. *Write the name and the abbreviation for your state and two nearby states.*

CLASSIFIEDS

Read the ad. The writer has made some mistakes with abbreviations. Use proofreading marks to correct the mistakes.

REMEMBER!

- Remember what you have learned about abbreviations.
- Remember the marks for capital and lowercase letters.
- Remember the marks for adding and taking away periods.
- Turn to page 5 if you need to review the marks.

Career Fair

Come to Career Fair at Clinton Elementary. You'll meet professionals from our community. You'll find out about interesting careers!

Clinton Elementary
989 Root Rd
Hot Springs, ar

wed
Mar 30, 2011
through
sat
apr 2, 2011
Hear different professionals every day!

Special appearances by the professionals listed below.

- ms Mata from Mata's Sporting Goods
- mr. Bedi from Accountants Group
- Ms Danic from the Danic Law Firm in San Antonio, tx
- dr Quell from Baton Rouge, La

Tickets will be available at the school and at Arty's Art Supplies at 651 Maple ave across the street from the mall.

Correctly rewrite the ad.

Career Fair

BOBCAT NEWS

NEWS

Read the article. The writer has made some mistakes with capital letters and abbreviations. Use proofreading marks to correct the mistakes.

REMEMBER!

- Remember what you have learned about capital letters and abbreviations.
- Remember the marks for capital and lowercase letters.
- Remember the marks for adding and taking away periods.
- Turn to page 5 if you need to review the marks.

Native Americans

by Jan Sola

We have been studying Native americans in our class. I have done so much research that i thought i would share some of the information in an article.

long before europeans came to north america, many different Tribes settled the land. One was the iroquois. The iroquois lived in the mountains of new york and pennsylvania.

Another tribe was the ojibwa. The ojibwa lived in michigan and other locations near the Great Lakes.

We also studied the lakota. The lakota were strong and powerful. they lived on the prairie in north dakota and south dakota.

in idaho, the Nez percé tribe was peaceful. many were traders and horse trainers.

If you want to learn more about Native americans, read the book <u>Early days In america</u>. My teacher, ms Walters, says, “this is one of the best Books about the topic.”

I shared this article with my Mother. I said, “Well, mom, you were right. this is a very interesting topic.”

A. *Correctly rewrite the article.*

B. *Circle the choice that shows correct capitalization and abbreviations.*

1. a. the first Thurs in Aug
   b. the first thurs. in Aug.
   c. the first Thurs. in Aug.
2. a. 4500 Prescott St. in Phoeniz, AZ
   b. 4500 Prescott st. in Phoeniz, AZ
   c. 4500 Prescott ST in Phoeniz, Az.
3. a. east Holton gymnastics group
   b. East Holton Gymnastics Group
   c. East holton gymnastics group
4. a. Irish and Italian cousins
   b. irish and Italian cousins
   c. Irish and italian cousins

COMICS

Read the comic. Use proofreading marks to correct capitalization and abbreviations.

Watery Treasure

by Oscar Zando

My Uncle sent me a birthday card. mom said i should wait to open it at the water park. I wonder why. Last week, my Uncle called and told me, "you're going to be surprised when you read your card. it will lead you to a treasure."

Wow! we had a special map in ms Beloit's class last year. It led us to a treasure. we had to carefully follow each step.

mr Liam Nelson
995 sycamore ave
orlando, fl.

Okay, let's see. first, go to the ride called the Giant wave. then, walk five steps to the right. next, walk to the stand with bottled water.

Hurry! i'm so excited!

i should read all the information carefully before we start.

Oh, No! It's wet!

Look, it is your Uncle! He can give you the clues you need to find your Birthday treasure!

Correctly rewrite the comic.

Watery Treasure

by Oscar Zando

LETTERS TO THE EDITOR

Read the letter to the editor. The writer has made some mistakes with end marks. Use proofreading marks to correct the mistakes.

REMEMBER!

- Use the correct end mark for each sentence type.
- Use a period to end a declarative sentence.
  We're going to the beach.
- Use a question mark to end an interrogative sentence.
  Did you go to the beach?
- Use a period to end most imperative sentences.
  Take some towels to the beach.
- Use an exclamation mark to end an exclamatory sentence.
  What a great day we had at the beach!
- Use these marks to add end marks.
  We're going to the beach ⊙
  Did you go to the beach ?‸
  What a great day to go to the beach !‸
- This is how you take out an end mark and add a new end mark.
  Did you go to the beach. ?‸

Journals

November 4, 2012

Dear Luisa,

Many of the students have been complaining about keeping a journal I think it is a wonderful idea to keep a journal.

It's easy to write in our journals about things we know? We can get ideas from family, friends, and school events What fun it will be to read our journals in twenty years? We will be able to read about so many of the things that happened to us?

Without a journal, do you think you would remember the day something crazy happened in the lunchroom. Would you enjoy reading about how proud you were when you worked hard and received a grade you really deserved

A journal will also help you with your writing for assignments? I hope everyone in fourth grade can get excited about keeping a journal.

Sincerely,

Wah Ling

Wah Ling

A. *Correctly rewrite the letter to the editor.*

____

____

____

____

____

____

____

____

____

____

____

____

____

____

B. *Write the correct end mark for each sentence.*

1. How old is your sister ______

2. What a fabulous time we had ______

3. Would you like to come to my party ______

4. The assignment is due on Wednesday ______

5. How wonderful it would be to run in the race ______

CLASSIFIEDS

Read this ad. The writer has made some mistakes with capital letters, abbreviations, and end marks. Use proofreading marks to correct the mistakes.

Mall Sale

All the stores in the mall will be part of the big sale

Check below for specific Information

Here is a letter from the mall president. she is one of our neighbors

Dear friends and neighbors,

we are so glad to be part of the Community. The Stores in the mall are happy to offer these special deals.

please come to share in good buys at the mall. What a good time you will have?

Your Neighbor,

Anya Dell

Melly Mall Sale

619 eastern ST.

Chicago, il.

Wed through Sun

Aug 31–SEPT 4

Do you want to be part of the best sale of the Summer. Come to Melly Mall. The Sale will end just before labor day. Come to eat and shop Our Restaurants have items from all over the world. You can buy french bread and mexican salsa. hope to see You at the sale!

Correctly rewrite the ad.

Mall Sale

LETTERS TO THE EDITOR

Read the letter to the editor. The writer has made some mistakes with commas. Use proofreading marks to correct the mistakes.

REMEMBER!

- Use a comma to separate the day and year in a date.
  March 5, 2012
- Use a comma to separate the name of a city from its state.
  Boise, Idaho
- Use a comma after the opening in a friendly letter, e-mail, or blog post to a friend.
  Dear Lina,
- Use a comma after first line in the closing of a letter, e-mail, or blog post.
  Sincerely,
  Mike
- Use this mark to add a comma.
  San Antonio, Texas
- Use this mark to take out a comma.
  April, 7, 2012

Sports Equipment

October 30 2012

Dear Juanita

I am writing this letter to interest other students and teachers in helping to raise money to buy new sports equipment.

Last night, I saw a school on the news. The school opened on August 12 2000. It was located in Dearborn Michigan. The principal explained that sports were an important part of the school day, and the parents and students raised quite a bit of money to buy extra sports equipment.

I know our school has many needs. I was happy about the new computers and new art supplies the school recently bought. But our school is located in Memphis Tennessee. We have warm weather throughout most of the school year. We could really use new kickball and volleyball equipment. Please meet me after school on Tuesday November 10 in the gym if you are interested in helping to raise money for more sports equipment. Thank you.

Sincerely

Nadia Cam

Nadia Cam

A. *Correctly rewrite the letter.*

B. *Circle the choice that shows correct use of commas.*

1. a. Paris France
   b. Rome, Italy
   c. London England,

2. a. December 12, 2013
   b. January 5 2011
   c. November, 3, 2012

3. a. Nome, Alaska
   b. Amarillo Texas
   c. Omaha Nebraska,

BOBCAT NEWS

STUDENT RECIPES

Read the recipe. The writer has made some mistakes with commas. Use proofreading marks to correct the mistakes.

REMEMBER!

- Use a comma after introductory words and phrases in a sentence.
  On Tuesday, your reports will be due at the beginning of class.
  Without a doubt, this is the best book I have read this year.
- Use a comma to separate three or more words in a series.
  Be sure to buy eggs, cheese, and bread.
- Remember the marks for adding and taking away commas. Turn to page 5 if you need to review the marks.

Recipe for Fruit Salad and Fun

by Faheem Elden

Last week I went to the lake to visit my aunt uncle and cousins. They have a house near the lake. We knew the drive would take about two hours, and we planned to spend the weekend. Before we left we packed snacks clothes and towels.

When we got to the lake everyone was happy to see us. My aunt cousins and my cousins' friends ran over to greet us. My aunt helped us unload the suitcases books and other items we had packed.

In the kitchen everyone was getting ready for lunch. I couldn't wait to help my dad make our family's favorite fruit salad. Here's how you make it.

First have an adult help you cut up watermelon pineapple and apples. Then drop coconut shreds in the bottom of a bowl. Next add raisins grapes watermelon pineapple and apples. Finally put more coconut shreds on top. Enjoy!

Correctly rewrite the recipe.

COMICS

Read the comic. Use proofreading marks to correct the mistakes with commas.

An Early Trip

by Gina Win

In New York City we'll visit the Empire State Building the Statue of Liberty and a pond in Central Park.

In my class we studied New York City.

We studied New York City in my class, too. We were studying transportation. We talked about planes trains and cars.

E-mail me while you're on your trip.

Sure I'll send you an e-mail. I also have to send e-mails to my grandma my neighbor and my teacher.
Hey did you hear the phone?
Yes that's probably the call I've been waiting for.

Well it looks like I didn't have to wait too long for my trip.
HA HA HA

Correctly rewrite the comic.

An Early Trip

by Gina Win

HA HA HA

Student Stories

Read the story. The writer has made some mistakes with commas. Use proofreading marks to correct the mistakes.

Remember!

- Use a comma after names in direct address in a sentence.
  "Reena, don't forget to feed the dog."
  "Dad, let's leave early today."
- Use a comma to separate a speaker's exact words from the other words in a sentence.
  He said, "I'd like to buy a new notebook."
  "I'd like to buy a new notebook," he said.

Works of Art

by Maureen Grundy

Ben rarely shared his art with others, but he was looking forward to the field trip to the art museum.

At the museum, students started at a sculpture room. The tour guide said "Ms. Anjal would you ask your students to look at the sculpture on the left?"

Ben looked at a sculpture by Rodin. He said to his friend "Ana that is the most amazing sculpture I've ever seen!"

As they continued through the museum, Ben saw something that fascinated him. "Look, Ana" he said. "There is some art work that looks like mine! I can't believe it!"

Ana and Ben read the information and listened to the tour guide. "The artist is Andy Warhol" said Ana. "Ben your art work really does look like his!"

The following week, Ben took two of his favorite pieces to share with the class. He was happy he'd found out that he wasn't the only artist with an unusual style.

A. *Correctly rewrite the story.*

B. *Circle the choice that shows correct use of commas.*

1. a. "Jonna let's go to the mall" said Lem.
   b. "Jonna, let's go to the mall" said Lem.
   c. "Jonna, let's go to the mall," said Lem.

2. a. I asked "Grandma, would you please bring me my scarf?"
   b. I asked, "Grandma, would you please bring me my scarf?"
   c. I asked, "Grandma would you please bring me my scarf?"

C. *Place commas correctly in these sentences.*

3. She asked "Dad when will we leave?"

4. "Misha please go with me" he said.

SUMMER BLOG POST

Read the blog post. The writer has made some mistakes with commas. Use proofreading marks to correct the mistakes.

Camping in Montana

August 10 2012

Dear Students

I had a wonderful summer on my family camping trip. My mom cousins and grandfather all went on the trip. We traveled to campgrounds near the city of Kalispell Montana. Well this was about the best trip I've ever taken!

On the trip I said "Mom the view here is amazing. I can't wait for our long hikes!" Afterward I said to my cousin "Abdul I was eager to go on the hike. Now I'm just exhausted!" Still we had a wonderful time!

Around the campfire we ate sang and visited. The sky was so clear, and we could hear sounds like chirping hooting and howling. At first one of my cousins was scared. But my mom told him we were safe.

Next year we plan to visit the city of Carlsbad New Mexico. One of the things we'll do is visit Carlsbad Caverns. I can't wait! Hope you've all had a good summer. Of course I'll see you in a couple of weeks.

Your friend

Annie

A. *Correctly rewrite the blog post.*

B. *Circle the choice that shows correct use of commas.*

1. a. Dear Mom, Dad, and Erin,

   b. Dear Mom Dad, and Erin

   c. Dear Mom Dad and Erin,

2. a. Your, cousin
   Abe

   b. Your cousin,
   Abe

   c. Your, cousin,
   Abe

3. a. We're ordering apples cheese, and pears.

   b. We're ordering apples, cheese, and pears.

   c. We're ordering apples cheese and, pears.

4. a. I said "Mark, this is the address."

   b. I said, "Mark this is the address."

   c. I said, "Mark, this is the address."

LETTERS TO THE EDITOR

Read the letter to the editor. The writer has made some mistakes with capital letters, abbreviations, end marks, and commas. Use proofreading marks to correct the mistakes.

REMEMBER!

- Remember what you have learned about capital letters, abbreviations, end marks, and commas.
- Remember the marks for capital letters.
- Remember the marks for adding and taking away end marks and commas.
- Turn to page 5 if you need to review the marks.

Favorite Book

Thurs May 2 2013

Dear Mikhail and newspaper staff

I was glad to see you asked for e-mails about favorite books Until now my favorite books were biographies novels and travel books. I just finished reading my first how-to Book. What an interesting book?

the Title is <u>How to Canoe</u>. the book was written by Dr Simonia Lakes. It includes text photos and drawings. Austin Tx. is the hometown of dr Lakes She likes to canoe near Jones AVE in austin.

Have you ever read a book that made you want to run out and try something Well that's how I felt after I finished this book. I said "Grandma will you canoe with us." She said "Mya I would love to take you on a canoeing trip." We're going next week, and i can't wait!

Best Wishes

Mya

Mya

A. *Correctly rewrite the letter.*

B. *Circle the correct answer choice.*

1. a. Wichita, KS and Nashville, TN
   b. Wichita, KS and Nashville, Tenn.
   c. Wichita, Kans. and Nashville, TN.
2. a. Ride elementary school computer club
   b. Ride elementary school Computer Club
   c. Ride Elementary School Computer Club
3. a. israeli, italian and swedish cities
   b. Israeli, Italian, and swedish cities
   c. Israeli, Italian, and Swedish cities
4. a. Mon., Mar. 18
   b. Fri, APR. 3
   c. Wed. Jan. 25

BOBCAT NEWS

NEWS

Read the article. The writer has made some mistakes with quotation marks. Use proofreading marks to correct the mistakes.

REMEMBER!

- Use quotation marks to separate a speaker's exact words from the other words in a sentence. Put the end mark inside the quotation marks.

  Padma said, "Snow is beginning to fall."

  Dan asked, "When is the report due?"

- Use this mark to add a quotation mark.

  Dan said, Let's go home."

- Use this mark to take away a quotation mark.

  "Dan said, "Let's go home."

School Greeting Cards

by José Juarez

The sale of greeting cards will be coming up next month. Ms. Ayoub says, This will be the biggest project for the spring. We hope everyone will help". Mr. Jonas says, "We need writers, artists, and students to make sales and pass out the cards

Students will write some of the cards. But some of the cards will be written by the senders. Donny Garza is in charge of the project. He says, "There will be a charge for writing and a separate charge for artwork".

I asked, How many cards were sent out last year? Donny explained that students sent almost 200 cards last year. "What a great year we had! he said.

A fifth grader told me, I hope we'll have even better sales this year"!

If you would like to sign up to help, go to the lunchroom after school on Thursday. Donny says, We will be offering refreshments and fun, so be sure to come!

A. *Correctly rewrite the article.*

B. *Write a brief article to tell about a school event or classroom discussion.*

- The article may be fiction or nonfiction.
- Include at least three quotes.
- Show quotation end marks of at least one period, one question mark, and one exclamation mark.

BOOK REVIEW

Read the book review. The writer has made some mistakes with quotation marks and underlining. Use proofreading marks to correct the mistakes.

REMEMBER!

- Use quotation marks for the title of a chapter.
  "How Bees Dance"
- Use quotation marks for the title of a song.
  "The Star-Spangled Banner"
- Use quotation marks for the title of a short story or play.
  "On Our Way"
- Use quotation marks for the title of a poem.
  "Stopping by Woods on a Snowy Evening"
- Underline the title of a book.
  A Wrinkle in Time
- Use this mark to add underlining.
  A Wrinkle in Time
  ^
- Remember the marks for adding and taking away quotation marks. Turn to page 5 if you need to review the marks.

Steps to the Treasure

by Porfiria Ang

I just finished reading a new book titled Steps to the Treasure. It was written by Benjamin Gade. This was an excellent book. After I read the first chapter, Day One of the Treasure Hunt, I couldn't put the book down.

The characters were very strong in the book, and the plot was really unusual. The characters had many lessons to learn as they solved the story problem. This book reminded me of the book Gulliver's Travels. The characters had to travel to many lands as they looked for the treasure.

The characters sang as they traveled. This helped them from feeling scared. One of the songs they sang was Merrily, We Roll Along.

Our teacher asked us to write poems about the books we read. We put our poems on posters. The title of my poem was The Treasure at the End of the Rainbow.

You can see my posters and other students' posters in the main hall. You'll learn more about all of the interesting books we've been reading!

A. *Correctly rewrite the book review.*

B. *Correctly write the title of one of each of the following. Do not include any of the titles from the book review.*

1. One of your favorite songs:
2. One of your favorite books:
3. One of your favorite poems:
4. A chapter from a book you have read:

CLASSIFIEDS

Read the ad. The writer has made some mistakes with capital letters, abbreviations, end marks, commas, quotation marks, and punctuation of titles. Use proofreading marks to correct the mistakes.

REMEMBER!

- Remember what you have learned about capital letters, abbreviations, end marks, commas, quotation marks, and punctuation of titles.
- Remember the marks you have learned. Turn to page 5 if you need to review the marks.

Chapter by Chapter

Chapter by Chapter is having A bookstore blowout sale! come to the finest bookstore in Town We promise You won't be disappointed. We sell sheet music books magazines and Plays. Our manager is ms sullivan She says, please let me know if you have any questions when you visit the store" Our customers say "this is the best bookstore in the City. we will have a great time shopping there"

This is Our Address.

491 venus RD

Aames Va.

these are some of Our sale Books.

the Wizard Of Oz

Madge And Nan

Spiders flies And ants

What a good selection of plays we have?

a Country divided

Tiana And The whale

Eleanor Of Aquitane

You'll find these short Stories in our Magazines and Books

my Favorite aunt

the Work To Build again

Back On The basketball Court

Correctly rewrite the ad.

Chapter by Chapter

BOBCAT NEWS

NEWS

Read the article. The writer has made some mistakes with apostrophes. Use proofreading marks to correct the mistakes.

REMEMBER!

- Use an apostrophe when two words are joined in a shortened form.

  did + not = didn't

  will + not = won't

- Use this mark to add an apostrophe.

  dont

- Use this mark to take away an apostrophe.

  do'n't

Possible Flooding

by Will Sanderson

Rain has been falling for a full week now. The river wont stop rising. Weve tried putting sandbags around the lake. Everyone is hoping the sandbags will help to keep the town from flooding.

We have'nt had a flood in our town since the 1950s. Most cant' even imagine what it would be like. The town is carefully preparing.

You shouldnt' be scared, though. There is a good chance the rain will stop soon, and the sandbags couldnt be stronger or set higher.

If the water doesnt stop rising tomorrow, school will be closed. We havent' ever had to do this, though. So, were thinking everything should be fine.

City officials cant say strongly enough that people shouldn't' be worried at this point. Were' all watching the news and the warnings. Next week, we hope well be able to print an article about the water level dropping.

A. *Correctly rewrite the article.*

B. *Circle the correct answer choice.*

1. a. We didn't know that they couldn't come.
   b. We didn't' know that they couldnt' come.
   c. We didnt' know that they could'nt come.
2. a. They shouldn't ask why were here.
   b. They shouldnt' ask why we're here.
   c. They shouldn't ask why we're here.
3. a. He can't tell where they'll go.
   b. He cant tell where they'll go.
   c. He can't tell where theyll go.
4. a. She has'nt explained how shell do it.
   b. She hasn't explained how she'll do it.
   c. She hasnt' explained how she'll do it.

CLASSIFIEDS

Read the ad. The writer has made some mistakes with apostrophes in possessive nouns. Use proofreading marks to correct the mistakes.

REMEMBER!

- Use a possessive noun to show that someone owns something.
- For most singular nouns, add an apostrophe and the letter *-s.*
  dog's dish
- For most plural nouns, add an apostrophe after the *-s.*
  dogs' dishes
- Remember the marks for adding and taking away apostrophes. Turn to page 5 if you need to review the marks.

Please! Help!

Jims' cats have disappeared. Their names are Kit and Kat. Kits' fur is brown. Kats' fur is black. Both cat's collars are purple.

Note from Jim:

My familys' house is near the park. The cats' dashed out our front door. All of our neighbors have been looking for the cats. Our neighbor's cries, all of them, have gone unanswered. We think the cats are still somewhere in the park. Thank you for your help!

This is the flyer Jims' dad has put up in Town Square.

Our cats' are missing. They disappeared on Monday, May 9. We last saw them near the park's sandbox. Please call us if you see them. 123-456-7891

Correctly rewrite the ad.

Please! Help!

SUMMER BLOG POSTS

Read the blog post. The writer has made some errors with capitalization and punctuation. Use proofreading marks to correct the mistakes.

REMEMBER!

Remember the marks for capitalization and punctuation. Turn to page 5 if you need to review the marks.

Underground Railroad

AUG 5 2013

Dear students

What an interesting trip we took last week? we went to see an old house near our town. Long ago it was a hiding place. it was a station on the underground railroad. When i walked inside i was amazed It was as though i had stepped back in time.

The person in charge was ms daily She told us all about the underground railroad. She said Many people were on their way to safety when they traveled."

I told my mother "You know mom this is better than any other trip we've taken. At the end of the tour we visited a shop at the front of the house. I bought a book titled "The way To Safety." My brother bought a poetry collection. his favorite poem in the collection is titled <u>Waiting For Freedom</u>, and the books cover is beautiful.

Next year i hope well get to visit again Until then i hope to continue to learn more about the Underground railroad

Your Friend

Naisha

Correctly rewrite the blog post.

CLASSIFIEDS

Read the ad. The writer has made some mistakes with pronouns. Use proofreading marks to correct the mistakes.

REMEMBER!

- The words *I, he, she, we,* and *they* are subjects. The word *you* can be a subject or an object.

  I am at school.

  You are in class.

  He is on the playground.

  She is in the gym.

  We are outside.

- The words *me, him, her, us,* and *them* are direct objects.

  Throw the ball to me.

  I will throw it to you.

  She is in the lunchroom with him.

  He is at school with her.

  They are in the car with us.

- Use these marks to take away one word and add another.

  ~~Him~~ He will give it to ~~they~~ them.

Help the School Bake Sale! A Note from Tim Fields: Student Head of Sales

Us need help with the school bake sale. Mr. Wong is the sponsor. Him has been working hard to plan the sale. Ms. Chastain is also helping with the sale. Her and Mr. Wong will both be happy to answer questions or take your name on the sign-up sheet.

Mr. Wong and me have spent time planning. Us have been helped by many other students. You and me can work together with other students to set up the tables.

Speak to Mr. Wong or Ms. Chastain if you want to help they with next year's sale. Them will be happy to tell you about next year's plans.

Correctly rewrite the ad.

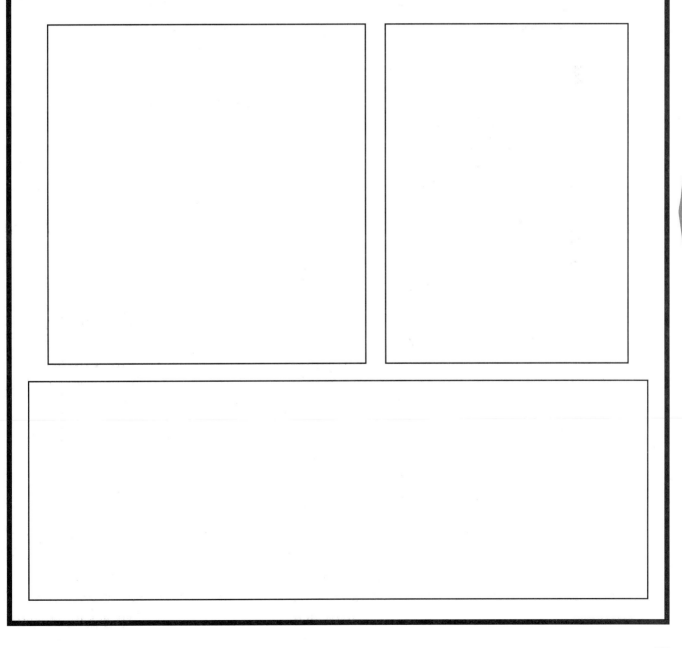

Help the School Bake Sale!
A Note from Tim Fields:
Student Head of Sales

Student Stories

Read the story. The writer has made some errors with double negatives. Use proofreading marks to take away incorrect words and add the correct words.

Remember!

- A negative word is a word that has a meaning like *no* or *not.*
  no not never nowhere nobody nothing
- Do not use double negatives, two negative words together. This includes negative contractions, such as:
  can't won't doesn't hadn't shouldn't didn't couldn't wouldn't
- Remember the marks for adding and taking away words. Turn to page 5 if you need to review the marks.

No Movies for Me?

by Lana Michaels

My friends didn't not want to stay home all day. It was raining. There wasn't not much to do. My friends asked if I wanted to go to the movies. I hadn't never seen the movie they were going to see, so I agreed to go. I couldn't hardly wait to meet my friends.

There's not nothing better than going to the movies on a rainy day. The movie theater is not nowhere near our neighborhood, so a parent had to drive.

We got to the theater. I reached into my bag. Oh, no! I couldn't find my money nowhere. The money wasn't nowhere to be found, and none of my friends didn't have enough money to loan to me. I thought I'd have to call someone to come pick me up and take me home.

Then one of my friends asked if I'd checked in the pocket of my jeans. I couldn't not believe it. But the money was way in the bottom of my pocket. I hadn't never been so embarrassed. Everyone laughed, and we all enjoyed the movie. I didn't never want to go through that again. I won't never again forget to check for my money before I leave home.

Correctly rewrite the story.

BOBCAT NEWS

NEWS

Read the article. The writer has confused some words. Use proofreading marks to correct the writer's mistakes.

REMEMBER!

Some words often confuse writers and readers. It is important to remember the correct spelling for each meaning of these words. Here are some examples.

your you're

their they're there

its it's

to too two

were we're where

here hear

who's whose

be bee

blue blew

cent scent sent

Book Donations

by Rick Pauls

A fire started in our town library last week. It burned the library to the ground. Your book donations are needed to help the library. The librarians say that they're needs include books of all kinds. They would like to receive magazines, to.

What will the future of the library bee? You can help two decide, and it won't cost you a sent. Just give old books you can spare.

"Were working around the clock," the head librarian told us. "You can bring your books hear to the grocery store. Its next door to the spot were the library used to be. Look for the store with the big green, read, and blew letters on the sign. Were collecting books back in the sail section."

Please give you're extra books. Everyone who donates will be a special guessed at a party when the library opens again. We don't know how many people will give. But we hope many will, sew the library can open again soon.

A. *Correctly rewrite the article.*

B. *Follow directions to write sentences below.*

1. On a separate sheet of paper, write two sentences about your neighborhood. Correctly use one of the words below in each sentence.

   who's whose

2. On a separate sheet of paper, write three sentences about your state. Correctly use one of the words below in each sentence.

   were we're where

Book Review

Read the book review. The writer has made some mistakes with adverbs and adjectives. Use proofreading marks to correct the mistakes.

Remember!

- Do not confuse adjectives and adverbs.
- Adjectives describe people, places, or things.
  He has a good friend.
- Adverbs can tell how, when, and where action happens.
  His friend speaks well.
- For most adjectives, add *-er* to compare two people, places, or things.
- For most adjectives, add *-est* to compare more than two people, places, or things.
- Use the word *good* to describe one person, place, or thing. Use the word *better* to describe two people places or things. Use the word *best* to describe three or more.

The Life of a Teacher

by Susan Prof

We had an assignment to read two books. One was fiction. The other was nonfiction. The nonfiction book I read was The Life of a Teacher. It was definitely the best of the two books. The author writes very good.

The book helped me understand how the life of one teacher was hardest than the lives of many others. He was the favoritest teacher in his school. He worked the harder of all the teachers. He prepared even gooder work than he had the year before.

This was an excellent book. It told about the teacher, and it also told about the teacher's bestest friend. The friend was the happier of all the people the teacher knew. She helped the teacher learn how to do an even gooder job every day.

I think everyone should read this book. It is about the wiser people I have ever read about in a book. It will make you think about the work of teachers. It will also help you think about how to make your own life gooder.

A. *Correctly rewrite the book review.*

B. *Circle the correct answer choice.*

1. a. He is my bestest friend.
   b. He is my goodest friend.
   c. He is my best friend.
2. a. She skates well.
   b. She skates good.
   c. She is a gooder skater than he is.
3. a. It is the nicer of all the dogs in the neighborhood.
   b. It is the nicest of all the dogs in the neighborhood.
   c. It is the most nicest of all the dogs in the neighborhood.
4. a. This pizza is better than the other one.
   b. This pizza is the best of the two pizzas.
   c. This pizza is the most best pizza of all the pizzas.

LETTERS TO THE EDITOR

Read the letter. The writer has made some spelling mistakes. Use proofreading marks to take away the misspelled words and add the correct words.

REMEMBER!

Correct spelling is important. There are some words that writers often spell incorrectly. Here are some examples.

already because could enough fierce
receive tonight trouble weather wrote

Practice will help you remember correct spelling.

Skool Speakers for Next Year

Deer Keisha,

I wuz glad the newspaper askt for ideas for nekst year's speekers. I wud like to have more peepul kome in to talk abowt and show animuls. Last yeer, we bot some hamsters for our class. They did not kost too much. Wee bot them with the monee we recieved from the bake sale. We have allready lurned so much abowt these animuls, and they are so kute.

I know everywon is really bizzy, but it wud be nice to arrange for snakes, spidurs, and other creatures to be shown to students. I have hurd that a groop in town gose to classes to show them.

I wud be hapy to save my pennys from change to giv to a fund to bring in these cretures. Neither of the fourth grade classes has seen these presentations. They wud be realy speshul. Becuz we want this so much, we hope it wil be posible.

It is quiet intereseting to lurn about new things. Some peepul thingk these critters are feirce, but I don't agre. I loook forwurd to reeding about othur students' ideas.

Sincerly,

Diana

Diana

A. *Correctly rewrite the letter.*

B. *Circle the answer choice in which all words are spelled correctly.*

1. a. wrote tonite adress
   b. untill tomorrow swiming
   c. first receive often
2. a. built February studying
   b. altho shure house
   c. truely cousin couldn't
3. a. carrys foxs arithmetic
   b. grade hellow height
   c. together making does
4. a. womens Wensday half
   b. weigh piece practice
   c. shugar early trouble

CLASSIFIEDS

Read the ad. The writer has made some spelling mistakes. Use proofreading marks to take away the misspelled words and add the correct words.

REMEMBER!

Remember the marks for adding and taking away letters and words. Turn to page 5 if you need to review the marks.

Garden Shop

Kome to our huje sale. You will not be disapointed. One of our kustomerz sez, "You culdn't finde a bedder deal anywere! It wud be a terribul shame to mis this sale!"

Wee hav flowerz for partys and all speshul events. Wee evun have a cuboard filled with tiny flowerz for hollidays.

Do you wunt to take sumthing to ur techur? We hav wut you need!

How doese our stor ofer such gud priceing? We groe the flowerz here! You kan walk throug our stor and see the garduns in the back of the bilding. Be our gest!

Correctly rewrite the ad.

Garden Shop

BOBCAT NEWS

NEWS

Read the article. The writer has made some mistakes with direct objects, negatives, comparison, and spelling. Use proofreading marks to correct the writer's mistakes.

REMEMBER!

Remember proofreading marks you have learned. Turn to page 5 if you need to review the marks.

Charles Lindbergh

by Ralph Voler

My freind and me went to the libray. I red a very gud article. It was one of the most goodest articles I have ever red. I hasn't never been so intrested in an article.

The article wuz abowt Charles Lindbergh. Flyeeng acrost the oshun in an airplain mite not seem unushual today. But that wuz not the case wen Lindbergh wuz in the air.

In 1927, Lindbergh flew akros the see. He landed in Paris. Nobody had never done this befour.

Lindbergh beleived that plains flying akrost an oshun wud bekum a vury importunt part uv transportashun. You no whut? He wuz write!

Twoday, plains fly to many countrys. They cary peepul. They cary items that hav bin sold. They delivur things that have bin cent to you and i.

Won day, I hope well be abul to fly up hi in a plain. Untill then, we kan dreem abowt it.

Correctly rewrite the article.

LETTERS TO THE EDITOR

Read the e-mail. The writer has made some mistakes with capital letters, punctuation, subject and object pronouns, negatives, spelling, and words to compare. Use proofreading marks to correct the writer's mistakes.

The Windy City

FRID Apr 2

To Michelle and the other editors,

I am happy you asked stoodents to rite about one of there most favoritest citys One of mine is chicago. you know my Mom and me visited this city last year. She said "this is a realy beeutiful place! I haven't never been nowhere so lovely.

do you no wat i lurnt abowt chicago. It is also known as the Windy City Why is this! Sum thingk its becuz their is sew much wind in the city. Its true that there is plenty uv wind. But this is knot the reezun for the name.

Long ago peepul told long tails about how wunderful the city wuz. They wanted chicago to be choosen as the place for the 1893 world's Fair. They sed so many theengs and spoke so much and fur such a long time that the citie got it's niknáme. It wuz sed two bee windy becuz of peepul talking and talking abowt the citie! i am glad i cud share this infurmashun with you.

A Chicago Fan

Monique

Correctly rewrite the e-mail.

STUDENT STORIES

Read the story. The writer made some mistakes with sentences. Use proofreading marks to correct the mistakes.

REMEMBER!

Sentences

- A sentence tells a complete thought. It includes a complete subject and a complete predicate.
  Sentence: The colorful fall leaves swirled to the ground.
- A fragment does not tell a complete thought. It does not include a complete subject and a complete predicate.
  Fragment: The colorful fall leaves.
  Fragment: Swirled to the ground.
- A run-on tells more than one complete thought. It must be broken into individual sentences.
  Run-on: The colorful fall leaves swirl to the ground they are lovely to watch.

The colorful fall leaves^ swirled to the ground

^Swirled to the ground. The colorful fall leaves

The colorful fall leaves swirl to the ground⊙ they are lovely to watch.

- Remember that a verb must agree with its subject.
  The teacher is in the lunchroom.
  Teachers are in the lunchroom.

Chugging Along

by Nan Trak

"All aboard!" the conductor yells, he are wearing a blue suit. Tina steps on board the train it are her first train ride. She find an empty seat, then she settles in for the long ride.

Tina are nervous, she sits near a window. Tina look out at the countryside.

Soon, Tina see farms and forests race by, the colors all blends together. Tina is less nervous now. She look at the other people on the train, they doesn't look nervous. Some is reading, some is talking.

The train ride finally end. Tina step carefully off of the train. She sees her grandmother, the two hug. Then they leaves the train station. Tina know this are going to be a wonderful vacation.

A. *Correctly rewrite the story.*

B. *Circle the answer choice that is a complete sentence.*

1. a. We will go.
   b. To the store.
   c. With our friends.

2. a. At the store.
   b. I plan to look.
   c. For a new notebook.

C. *Fill in the answer choice that shows correct subject-verb agreement.*

3. a. She and her friend tries something new.
   b. All of them works together on the poster.
   c. Her friend and his dad bring the markers.

4. a. He and I write the report.
   b. Someone else create the drawings.
   c. The teachers and students likes the poster.

Bobcat News

News

Read the article. The writer has written the whole article as one long paragraph, and many of the sentences are short and choppy. Use proofreading marks to combine sentences and to show where each new paragraph should start.

Remember!

- Every idea in a paragraph should tell about the topic, or main idea, of the paragraph. New paragraphs are important in making writing interesting and clear.
- Use this mark to show where a new paragraph should begin.

- It is important to write sentences that flow. Sometimes, it is necessary to combine sentences to improve the flow of a paragraph.

  The storm brought rain. The storm brought wind. The storm brought lightning.

  The storm brought rain, wind, and lightning.

Author Speaks to Students

by Bill Cramer

Author Keith Bhagwat came to speak to students last Wednesday. The author is also a chef. He wrote a book about his favorite recipes. The book explains how he learned to be a chef. The book explains where he learned to be a chef. The book explains why he decided to learn to be a chef. First, Mr. Bhagwat discussed his childhood. His dad was a chef. His mom was a chef. His uncle was a chef. So, he was around cooking from the time he was very young. Next, Mr. Bhagwat told us about the kinds of dishes he enjoys cooking. He enjoys cooking with vegetables. He enjoys cooking with spices. He enjoys cooking with noodles. He has enjoyed cooking with these ingredients for a long time. Finally, Mr. Bhagwat let us taste one of his most famous dishes. It was delicious! Everyone was very happy to have a sample. After Mr. Bhagwat finished speaking, he autographed copies of one of his recipes for us. We all hope he'll come back to our school again soon.

A. *Correctly rewrite the article.*

B. *Explain how you decided where it was necessary to start new paragraphs.*

BOOK REVIEW

Read the book review. The writer has made some mistakes. Use proofreading marks to correct the writer's mistakes.

REMEMBER!

- Remember what you have learned about capital letters, punctuation, subject and object pronouns, negatives, spelling, and words to compare.
- Remember what you have learned about subject-verb agreement, complete sentences, and paragraphs.
- Remember proofreading marks you have learned. Turn to page 5 if you need to review the marks.

A Wrinkle in Time

by Cheena Amra

In this Book a Sister and Brother travel threw tim and space. They no they must save they're Father. It wuz nice that the Author let the children solve the problems in the book. They're action really makes you want to reed more.

This is a gud exampul of science fiction. It pulls in the Reader's interest from the first moment. I wont give away the meaning of the Title of the book. but i say "friends you shud read this book. What an ending? After reading youll be able to understand the title. You mite even want to right science fiction for you're next assignment.

MR Danel recommended A wrinkle In time two me. And i strongly recommend it too you. it is one of the finest books I have evur red. This book was written by madeleine L'Engle. She writes descriptions that make you feel as though you are traveling threw time write along with the characters.

You shud reed this book. Its excellent!

Correctly rewrite the book review.

STUDENT STORIES

Read the story. The writer has made some mistakes. Use proofreading marks to correct the writer's mistakes. Be sure to separate the story into paragraphs.

What a Visit!

by alan Kang

One sumer, my Cousin dave kame to stay with us. It were the baddest summer of my life? There wasn't never a badder time. What a dificult visit? Won day, Dave say that we was al going in the lake on a bote. Wat happund in the watur? the bote started too singk. Their we're wholes in the bottom, we had to swim to shor. the nexst day were tuseday. Dave decided two go too the curcus. he say "pleeze kum with me." And we did. But he took us to the rong place. We had to walk al the way bak home. On wensday, dave say we shud all go hikeing, the hike was realy long. Gues whut hapunt. We akcidentully stept in poison ivy. Whut will we do nekst sumer. Im not shure. But i no i wont' lissen to dave!

Correctly rewrite the story.

Read the comic. Use proofreading marks to correct the mistakes.

How Can You Lose Something That's Already Lost?

by Dana Boneil

i lost my tooth!
i no you lost ur tooth. Why does that make you sad. You no you always gets a surprize when you loose a tooth.

No i really lost my tooth.
Wut do you mean

i put my tooth in the speshul box. Its the box were i allways put a lost tooth. and then i lost the tooth box!

Pleeze help me find it!

Ill' help you luk for it. The too of us, well look evurywere.

TOYS
Well we found it!
Yes. You allmost had the cleenest, lost, lost tooth in Town!

Correctly rewrite the comic.

How Can You Lose Something That's Already Lost?

by Dana Boneil

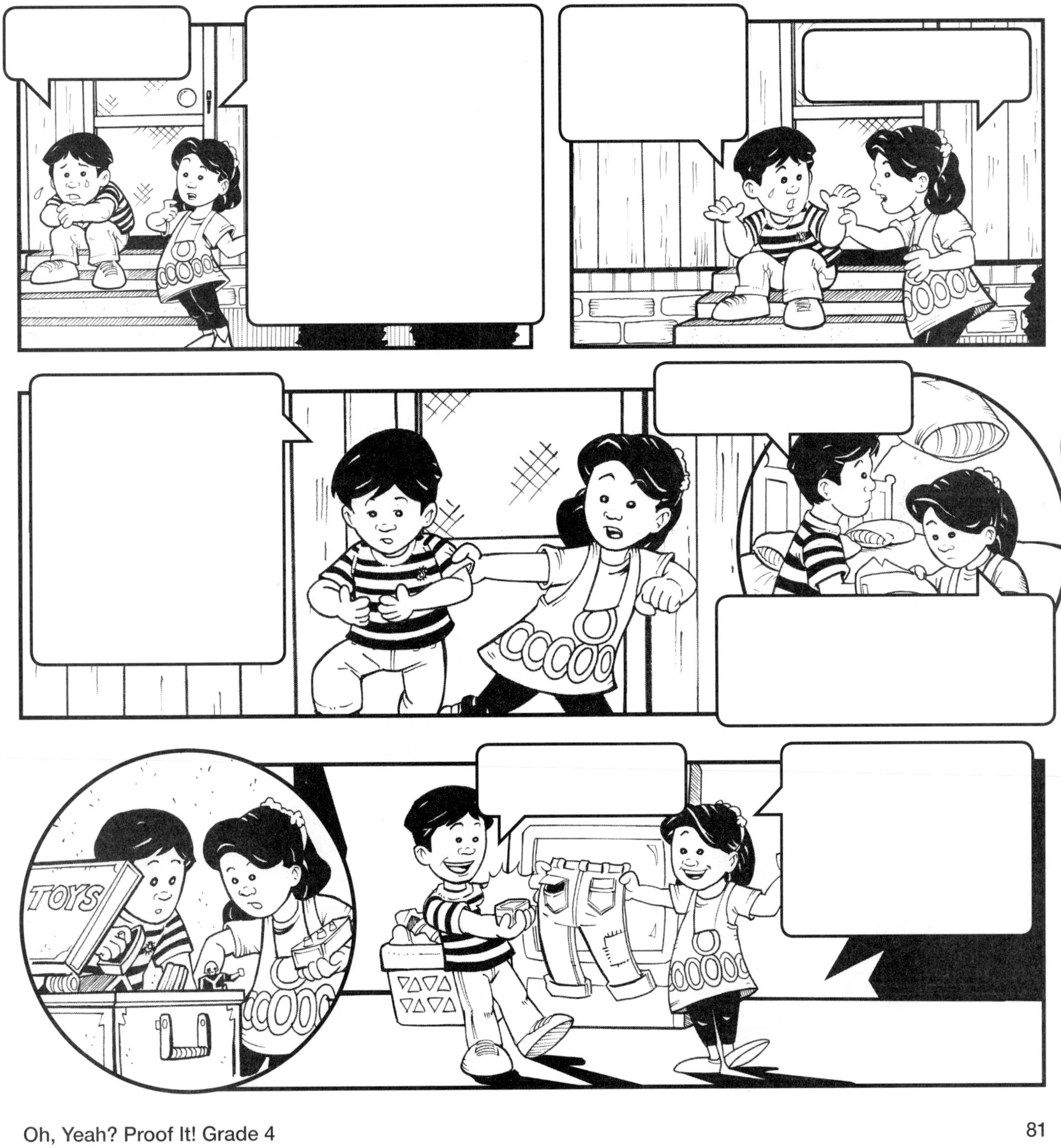

CLASSIFIEDS

Read the ad. A student made some mistakes while typing the ad. Use proofreading marks to correct the student's mistakes.

REMEMBER!

Remember the proofreading marks you have learned. Turn to page 5 if you need to review the marks.

Art Show

May 1 2012

Dear students familys and friends

We invite al uv you to kome to the skool art show, it will bee held on Wed and thurs evenings. students has bin wurking very hard to prepare. I haven't never seen a class work harder. This is one of the bestest art shows we has evur had. If posibul pleeze trie to kome urly on wed nite, i look forwurd two seing you their.

Your Principal

Dr Riang

Painteengs are based on the book poem song and storys belowe.

- Book: "The life And times Of A skater in denver Col"
- Poem: Waching aprul showers And Waiting For spring flours
- Song: Truble In River Citie
- Storys:

<u>Waiting For Tomorow And A Day</u> <u>a Lessun For Peace In The Wurld</u>

Correctly rewrite the ad.

Art Show

has made some mistakes with capital letters. Use proofreading marks to correct the mistakes.

names a person, place, or thing.
Common Nouns: child, town, pet
- A proper noun begins with a capital letter and names a specific person, place, or thing.
Proper Nouns: Jan, Seattle, Muffy
- This is how you show a change from a capital letter to a lowercase letter.
Child
- This is how you show a change from a lowercase letter to a capital letter.
seattle

Car Wash

by Sue Mcfta

The car wash at nearby jefferson high school was a great success. It gave us many Ideas for our own school car Wash next Year. My Sister, anya, was in charge of the event.

many hours of planning went into the event. students put up posters in Stores across the city. They handed out coupons at a local Floral shop named flowers are us. students also found a bakery, jake's cakes, to give refreshments for the workers.

to prepare, Students set up soap, Buckets, hoses, Gloves, and rags. they used a special kind of soap that is not bad for the Environment. drivers entered through the South entrance of the parking lot. three Students worked on each Car to wash, rinse, and dry It.

Almost sixty Cars were washed. students worked in shifts of two Hours. there were plenty of students to help. many Family members and Teachers helped.

At the end of the Day, students were tired, and the Parking Lot at the High School was very soapy! students cleaned up everything and looked forward to Events that would be possible because of Money from the car wash.

6 Oh Yeah? Proof It! Grade 4

page 6

A. *Correctly rewrite the article.*

Car Wash

by Sue Mcfta

The car wash at nearby Jefferson High School was a great success. It gave us many ideas for our own school car wash next year. My sister, Anya, was in charge of the event.

Many hours of planning went into the event. Students put up posters in stores across the city. They handed out coupons at a local floral shop named Flowers Are Us. Students also found a bakery, Jake's Cakes, to give refreshments for the workers.

To prepare, students set up soap, buckets, hoses, gloves, and rags. They used a special kind of soap that is not bad for the environment. Drivers entered through the south entrance of the parking lot. Three students worked on each car to wash, rinse, and dry it.

Almost sixty cars were washed. Students worked in shifts of two hours. There were plenty of students to help. Many family members and teachers also helped.

At the end of the day, students were tired, and the parking lot at the high school was very soapy! Students cleaned up everything and looked forward to events that would be possible because of money from the car wash.

B. Student's article should include correct capitalization, as well as information about a city and names of people.

B. *Write an article of your own on a separate piece of paper.*

- [ ] Include an article title and your name.
- [ ] Tell something interesting about a city you have visited—or would like to visit.

page 7

has made some mistakes with capital letters. Use proofreading marks to correct the mistakes.

letter.
He asked his mom if he could stay longer.
He asked, "Mom, may I stay longer?"
I'd like to wish you a very happy birthday,
Mom.
- Remember the rules you have learned about capital letters.
- Remember the marks for capital and lowercase letters. Turn to page 5 if you need to review the marks.

To Play or Not to Play?

by Tim Strang

Hakeem preferred to spend more time playing the Piano than doing almost anything else. the thought of playing in front of others made him shake and quake. His Dad would often ask, "hakeem, wouldn't you like to play piano at school?"

Hakeem would always give the same answer. "You know, dad, that i am too scared to play in front of the school. What if i make a mistake?"

At school the following week, hakeem's Sister walked over. "We have a chance to win new computers for the School. There's a music competition. I told grandpa just last week that i think you are one of the best piano Players i have ever heard. Will You do it?"

Hakeem just hung his head and walked away. Then, ms. chang stopped Him in the hall. she'd heard about how well he played. she told him, "Our school computers have gotten really old. Please, will You play in the competition?"

Hakeem's heart raced. But He knew what He had to do. He agreed to help his School.

8 Oh Yeah? Proof It! Grade 4

page 8

To Play or Not to Play?

by Tim Strang

Hakeem preferred to spend more time playing the piano than doing almost anything else. The thought of playing in front of others made him shake and quake. His dad would often ask, "Hakeem, wouldn't you like to play piano at school?"

Hakeem would always give the same answer. "You know, Dad, that I am too scared to play in front of the school. What if I make a mistake?"

At school the following week, Hakeem's sister walked over. "We have a chance to win new computers for the school. There's a music competition. I told Grandpa just last week that I think you are one of the best piano players I have ever heard. Will you do it?"

Hakeem just hung his head and walked away. Then, Ms. Chang stopped him in the hall. She'd heard about how well he played. She told him, "Our school computers have gotten really old. Please, will you play in the competition?"

Hakeem's heart raced. But he knew what he had to do. He agreed to help his school.

B. *Use proofreading marks to correct the mistakes with capitals in the sentences below.*

1. Did You know that i asked my Mom for a new pair of skates?
2. he said, "Please help me, grandma."
3. She gave the report to her Teacher, mr. Ling.
4. My Dad and i will go to dinner at the Restaurant.

page 9

Turn to page 5 if you need to review the marks.

Giant Sale at Skate Time

You won't believe the deals you'll find at skate time! be sure to cut out the coupon at the bottom of the page. You can use it only on Friday, may 1.

Sale Dates

thursday, april 30 wednesday, may 5

We won't have another sale until the Day after thanksgiving, so get the good deals now!

Big, Big Specials

On friday, all helmets will be half price.

all skates will be half price on saturday.

you can buy all skate Books for half price on monday.

Use this coupon on friday, may 1.

This coupon is good on one Day only. bring it in to receive $1.00 off of any purchase.

10 Oh Yeah? Proof It! Grade 4

page 10

Giant Sale at Skate Time

You won't believe the deals you'll find at Skate Time! Be sure to cut out the coupon at the bottom of the page. You can use it only on Friday, May 1.

Sale Dates

Thursday, April 30 Wednesday, May 5

We won't have another sale until the day after Thanksgiving, so get the good deals now!

Big, Big Specials

On Friday, all helmets will be half price.

All skates will be half price on Saturday.

You can buy all skate books for half price on Monday.

Use this coupon on Friday, May 1.

This coupon is good on one day only. Bring it in to receive $1.00 off of any purchase.

page 11

Answer Key

Paris

451 King ...
Oshkosh, WI

• Use a capital letter to begin a proper adjective.
Italian Polish Swedish

Dear Ms. Jula:

We have been studying many cultures. Our teacher has asked us to write letters to the editor to explain what we learned about other Countries. My cousin and my aunt and uncle are french. They live in paris, france. My dad and I went to visit them last year.

The plane ride was almost ten hours long! While we were on the plane, small screens showed a Map. A little airplane on the Map showed where we were. I could see the locations of many of the Countries we have studied. I saw england, italy, france, and many other Countries.

In paris, we visited the eiffel tower and went to Museums, Palaces, and Gardens. Many people walk and take the metro in paris. The metro is sort of like the subway in new york. Most of the cars on the Street are very small, and there are not very many places to park.

My dad has friends who are irish and italian. We wanted to visit ireland and italy on our trip, but we didn't have enough time. My report and other students' reports will be posted in the hall near the fourth grade classrooms. We hope students will come by to read the reports and see the pictures.

Sincerely,

Nia Lang

Nia Lang

12 Oh Yeah? Proof It! Grade 4

page 12

Paris

Dear Ms. Jula:

We have been studying many cultures. Our teacher has asked us to write letters to the editor to explain what we learned about other countries. My cousin and my aunt and uncle are French. They live in Paris, France. My dad and I went to visit them last year.

The plane ride was almost ten hours long! While we were on the plane, small screens showed a map. A little airplane on the map showed where we were. I could see the locations of many of the countries we have studied. I saw England, Italy, France, and many other countries.

In Paris, we visited the Eiffel Tower and went to museums, palaces, and gardens. Many people walk and take the metro in Paris. The metro is sort of like the subway in New York. Most of the cars on the street are very small, and there are not very many places to park.

My dad has friends who are Irish and Italian. We wanted to visit Ireland and Italy on our trip, but we didn't have enough time. My report and other students' reports will be posted in the hall near the fourth grade classrooms. We hope students will come by to read the reports and see the pictures.

Sincerely,

Nia Lang

B. *Circle the address that is correctly capitalized. Then, use proofreading marks to correct the addresses that are not correct.*

234 jones Road Houston, Tx	599 Oak Lane New Orleans, LA	922 Rula Avenue San Diego, ca	710 silas Street Philadelphia, PA

page 13

Damaged Backpacks

closing of letter
Your good friend,
Your grandson,

• Remember the marks for capital and lowercase letters. Turn to page 5 if you need to review the marks.

To My school friends,

One of the teachers and I ordered backpacks for members of the Camp scouts of America at our school. The backpacks arrived. They were all damaged. They had broken zippers, broken clips, and tears.

I tried to call the company, but no one would help on the phone. I finally sent a letter to the company owner. I explained that we had decided to order from the company because the Society for the prevention of cruelty to Animals had ordered from the same Web site. The people there said the items they received were in excellent condition.

I explained that we liked the look and size of the backpacks. But I also explained all the problems. I told them we'd planned to order from the Company again next year, but we needed these backpacks replaced. Guess what? They sent us new ones! If anyone from the Franklin elementary School drama Club or another club wants to order from the company, I'll give you the information.

Your Friend,

Nanette Lapour

14 Oh Yeah? Proof It! Grade 4

page 14

Write a short blog post to a friend or your class. Explain how you solved a problem. Include a greeting and a closing.

Blog posts will vary. Each post should explain how a problem was solved. It should be written to a friend or a class. The post should include a greeting and a closing, as well as correct capitalization in greeting and closing and correct mechanics throughout.

page 15

Resources for Reports

Treasure Island
The Cricket in Times Square

• Use a capital letter for the first word in a quotation.
My brother said, "Let's get ready for the party."

• Remember the marks for capital and lowercase letters. Turn to page 5 if you need to review the marks.

At the beginning of the school year, teachers post a list of good resources for your research reports in the school newspaper. The list for fourth grade is posted here. Additions to the list will be made later. Mr. Lyle says, "our resources this year are very strong." Ms. Halda says, "please speak to one of your own teachers if you have questions about these resources."

Resource List

Books	Songs
Biography Of Frederick Douglass	"the country's Banner"
the beginning of America	"stars And stripes forever"
Susan B. Anthony And Women's rights	"trying To Begin Our lives In A new Place"
Plays	**Poems**
an Author's world	"afternoon On a Hill"
the Wizard Of oz	"Stopping By Woods on A Snowy evening"
A Bull In A China Shop	"Looking up At The snowy peaks"

16 Oh Yeah? Proof It! Grade 4

page 16

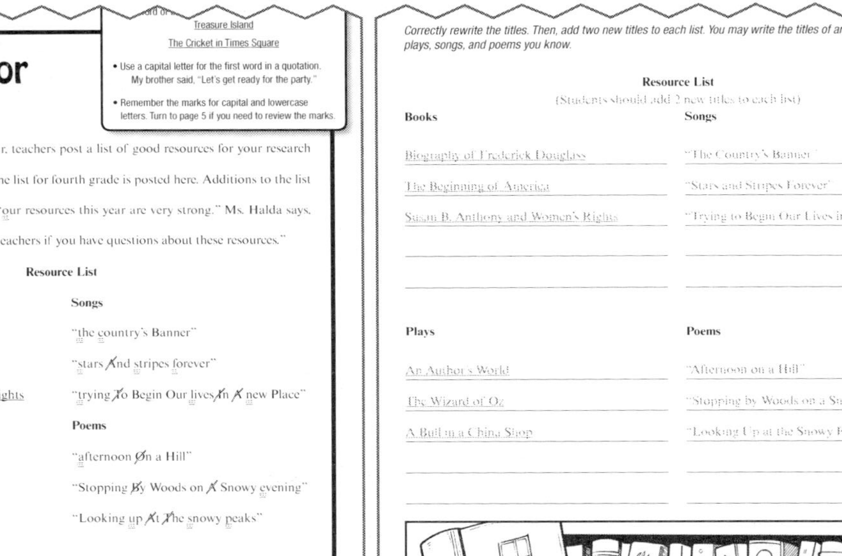

Correctly rewrite the titles. Then, add two new titles to each list. You may write the titles of any books, plays, songs, and poems you know.

Resource List
(Students should add 2 new titles to each list)

Books	Songs
Biography of Frederick Douglass	"The Country's Banner"
The Beginning of America	"Stars and Stripes Forever"
Susan B. Anthony and Women's Rights	"Trying to Begin Our Lives in a New Place"
Plays	**Poems**
An Author's World	"Afternoon on a Hill"
The Wizard of Oz	"Stopping by Woods on a Snowy Evening"
A Bull in a China Shop	"Looking Up at the Snowy Peaks"

page 17

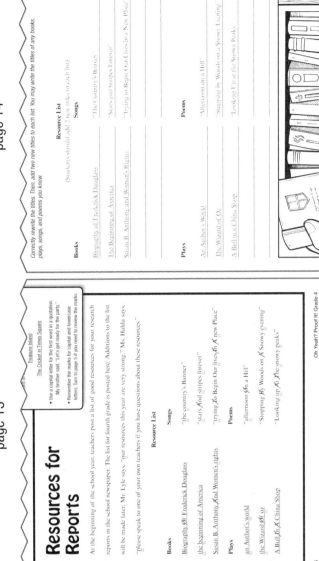

A Wrinkle in Time

In this Book, a Sister and Brother travel through time and space. they know they must save their Father. It was nice that the Author let the Sister and Brother solve the problems in the book.

This is a strong example of science fiction. it catches the Reader's interest from the first moment, and it is interesting from beginning to end. I won't give away the meaning of the title of the Book, but i would urge everyone to read it to figure out what the title means.

I would strongly recommend A wrinkle in time. It is one of the finest books I have ever read. This book was written by madeleine L'Engle. she writes descriptions that make you feel as though you are traveling through time right along with the characters.

The plot in this Book is strong. The action draws in the reader, and then the action builds and builds. Without a doubt, i recommend this book.

18 Oh Yeah? Proof It! Grade 4

page 18

A Wrinkle in Time

In this book, a sister and brother travel through time and space. They know they must save their father. It was nice that the author let the sister and brother solve the problems in the book.

This is a strong example of science fiction. It catches the reader's interest from the first moment and it is interesting from beginning to end. I won't give away the meaning of the title of the book, but I would urge everyone to read it to figure out what the title means.

I would strongly recommend A Wrinkle in Time. It is one of the finest books I have ever read. This book was written by Madeleine L'Engle. She writes descriptions that make you feel as though you are traveling through time right along with the characters.

The plot in this book is strong. The action draws in the reader, and then the action builds and builds. Without a doubt, I recommend this book.

B. *Circle the choice that shows correct capitalization.*

1. a. Dr. mitchell and Mr. Ganesh
   (b) Dr. Mitchell and Mr. Ganesh
   c. dr. mitchell and Mr. Ganesh
2. (a) He asked, "Dad, could we go to see a movie?"
   b. He asked, "dad, could we go to see a movie?"
   c. he asked, "dad, could we go to see a movie?"
3. (a) French and Russian cultures
   b. french and Russian cultures
   c. French and russian cultures
4. a. Girl scouts of America
   (b) Girl Scouts of America
   c. Girl Scouts of america
5. a. Ms. Rald dawson 422 Gatsby Lane
   (b) Ms. Rald Dawson 422 Gatsby Lane
   c. Ms. Rald Dawson 422 Gatsby Lane

page 19

Important Fall Events

- Use this mark to add a period if it is missing. Tues
- Use this mark to take away a period that does not belong. TX
- Remember the marks for capital and lowercase letters.

- Drama Club will meet on wed after school every week. See ms Bhatt for more information.
- Science Club will meet on thurs before school every week. The advisor is dr Johnston.
- Meetings to prepare for the winter fundraiser will be held on the last mon in aug and the first mon in sept this fall. Ms Wu is in charge.
- The orchestra will meet before school on tues through fri in the band room. Talk to ms Lang if you have questions.
- Chorus members will meet after school on wed and thurs each week. For more information, see mr Abraham.
- Planning for the fall fair will be held on each mon during the month of oct at school. The room number for the meetings will be posted later.
- We will post more fall information in upcoming issues. We will post information for the spring in the jan issue of the newspaper. Send an e-mail to Ms Sloan if you have items to be included.

20 Oh Yeah? Proof It! Grade 4

page 20

A. *Write a list of your classes or activities for three months. Include at least six activities on the list. Abbreviate all months and days of the week. Include abbreviations for at least five days of the week and three months.*

Answers will vary, but should include at least six activities, each with a day of the week and month of the year. All days and months should be correctly abbreviated.

B. *Write the names of five teachers you have now or have had in the past. Write the name of a doctor whose name you have seen or heard. Use abbreviations for the people's titles.*

Answers will vary, but should include names of five of the student's current or past teachers, as well as the name of a doctor. All titles should be correctly abbreviated.

C. *Write the name and the abbreviation for your state and two nearby states.*

Student should include the name and postal abbreviation for student's state, as well as names and postal abbreviations for two nearby states.

page 21

Career Fair

Come to Career Fair at Clinton Elementary. You'll meet professionals from our community. You'll find out about interesting careers!

Clinton Elementary
989 Root Rd
Hot Springs, ar

wed
Mar 30, 2011
through
sat
apr 2, 2011
Hear different professionals every day!

Special appearances by the professionals listed below.

- ms Mata from Mata's Sporting Goods
- mr. Bedi from Accountants Group
- Ms Danic from the Danic Law Firm in San Antonio, tx
- dr Quell from Baton Rouge, La

Tickets will be available at the school and at Arty's Art Supplies at 651 Maple ave across the street from the mall.

22 Oh Yeah? Proof It! Grade 4

page 22

Career Fair

Come to Career Fair at Clinton Elementary. You'll meet professionals from our community. You'll find out about interesting careers!

Clinton Elementary
989 Root Rd
Hot Springs, AR

Wed.
Mar. 30, 2011
through
Sat.
Apr. 2, 2011
Hear different professionals every day!

Special appearances by the professionals listed below.

- Ms. Mata from Mata's Sporting Goods
- Mr. Bedi from Accountants Group
- Ms. Danic from the Danic Law Firm in San Antonio, TX
- Dr. Quell from Baton Rouge, LA

Tickets will be available at the school and at Arty's Art Supplies at 651 Maple Ave. across the street from the mall.

page 23

Answer Key

page 24

page 25

B. Circle the choice that shows correct capitalization and abbreviations.

1. a. the first Thurs in Aug
   b. the first thurs. in Aug.
   c. (circled) the first Thurs. in Aug.
2. a. (circled) 4500 Prescott St. in Phoenix, AZ
   b. 4500 Prescott st. in Phoeniz, AZ
3. a. east Holton gymnastics group
   b. (circled) East Holton Gymnastics Group
   c. East holton gymnastics group
4. a. (circled) Irish and Italian cousins
   b. irish and Italian cousins

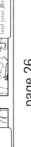

page 26

page 27

page 28

page 29

B. 1. ?
2. !
3. ?
4. .
5. !

ANSWER KEY

Mall Sale

All the stores in the mall will be part of the big sale, on !

Check below for specific information.

Here is a letter from the mall president. she is one of our neighbors.

Dear friends and neighbors,

we are so glad to be part of the community. The stores in the mall are happy to offer these special deals.

please come to share in good buys at the mall. What a good time you will have!

Your Neighbor,

Anya Dell

Melly Mall Sale
619 eastern St.
Chicago, il
Wed through Sun
Aug 31 SEPT 4

Do you want to be part of the best sale of the Summer? Come to Melly Mall. The Sale will end just before labor day. Come to eat and shop. Our Restaurants have items from all over the world. You can buy french bread and mexican salsa. hope to see You at the sale!

30 Oh Yeah? Proof It! Grade 4

page 30

Mall Sale

page 31

Sports Equipment

- Use a comma after the opening in a friendly letter, e-mail, or blog post to a friend.
  Dear Lina,
- Use a comma after first line in the closing of a letter, e-mail, or blog post.
  Sincerely,
  Mike
- Use this mark to add a comma.
  San Antonio, Texas
- Use this mark to take out a comma.
  April 7, 2012

October 30, 2012

Dear Juanita,

I am writing this letter to interest other students and teachers in helping to raise money to buy new sports equipment.

Last night, I saw a school on the news. The school opened on August 12, 2000. It was located in Dearborn, Michigan. The principal explained that sports were an important part of the school day, and the parents and students raised quite a bit of money to buy extra sports equipment.

I know our school has many needs. I was happy about the new computers and new art supplies the school recently bought. But our school is located in Memphis, Tennessee. We have warm weather throughout most of the school year. We could really use new kickball and volleyball equipment. Please meet me after school on Tuesday, November 10 in the gym if you are interested in helping to raise money for more sports equipment. Thank you.

Sincerely,

Nadia Cam

Nadia Cam

32 Oh Yeah? Proof It! Grade 4

page 32

B. 1. b
2. a
3. a

page 33

has made some mistakes with commas. Use proofreading marks to correct the mistakes.

- Use a comma after introductory words and phrases in a sentence.
  On Tuesday, your reports will be due at the beginning of class.
  Without a doubt, this is the best book I have read this year.
- Use a comma to separate three or more words in a series.
  Be sure to buy eggs, cheese, and bread.
- Remember the marks for adding and taking away commas. Turn to page 5 if you need to review the marks.

Recipe for Fruit Salad and Fun

by Faheem Elden

Last week, I went to the lake to visit my aunt, uncle, and cousins. They have a house near the lake. We knew the drive would take about two hours, and we planned to spend the weekend. Before we left, we packed snacks, clothes, and towels.

When we got to the lake, everyone was happy to see us. My aunt, cousins, and my cousins' friends ran over to greet us. My aunt helped us unload the suitcases, books, and other items we had packed.

In the kitchen, everyone was getting ready for lunch. I couldn't wait to help my dad make our family's favorite fruit salad. Here's how you make it.

First, have an adult help you cut up watermelon, pineapple, and apples. Then, drop coconut shreds in the bottom of a bowl. Next, add raisins, grapes, watermelon, pineapple, and apples. Finally, put more coconut shreds on top. Enjoy!

34 Oh Yeah? Proof It! Grade 4

page 34

Correctly rewrite the recipe.

page 35

Answer Key

page 36

page 37

Read the story. The writer has made some mistakes with commas. Use proofreading marks to correct the mistakes.

REMEMBER!

- Use a comma after names in direct address in a sentence.
  "Reena, don't forget to feed the dog."
  "Dad, let's leave early today."
- Use a comma to separate a speaker's exact words from the other words in a sentence.
  He said, "I'd like to buy a new notebook."
  "I'd like to buy a new notebook," he said.

Works of Art

by Maureen Grundy

Ben rarely shared his art with others, but he was looking forward to the field trip to the art museum.

At the museum, students started at a sculpture room. The tour guide said, "Ms. Anjal, would you ask your students to look at the sculpture on the left?"

Ben looked at a sculpture by Rodin. He said to his friend, "Ana, that is the most amazing sculpture I've ever seen!"

As they continued through the museum, Ben saw something that fascinated him. "Look, Ana," he said. "There is some art work that looks like mine! I can't believe it!"

Ana and Ben read the information and listened to the tour guide. "The artist is Andy Warhol," said Ana. "Ben, your art work really does look like his!"

The following week, Ben took two of his favorite pieces to share with the class. He was happy he'd found out that he wasn't the only artist with an unusual style.

page 38

B. 1. c **2. b**

C. *Place commas correctly in these sentences.*

3. She asked, "Dad, when will we leave?"
4. "Misha, please go with me," he said.

Oh Yeah? Proof It! Grade 4 39

page 39

Camping in Montana

August 10, 2012

Dear Students,

I had a wonderful summer on my family camping trip. My mom, cousins, and grandfather all went on the trip. We traveled to campgrounds near the city of Kalispell, Montana. Well, this was about the best trip I've ever taken!

On the trip, I said, "Mom, the view here is amazing. I can't wait for our long hikes!" Afterward, I said to my cousin, "Abdul, I was eager to go on the hike. Now, I'm just exhausted!" Still, we had a wonderful time!

Around the campfire, we ate, sang, and visited. The sky was so clear, and we could hear sounds like chirping, hooting, and howling. At first, one of my cousins was scared. But my mom told him we were safe.

Next year, we plan to visit the city of Carlsbad, New Mexico. One of the things we'll do is visit Carlsbad Caverns. I can't wait! Hope you've all had a good summer. Of course, I'll see you in a couple of weeks.

Your friend,

Annie

40 Oh Yeah? Proof It! Grade 4

page 40

B. *Circle the choice that shows correct use of commas.*

1. (a) Dear Mom, Dad, and Erin,
   b. Dear Mom Dad, and Erin
   c. Dear Mom Dad and Erin,
2. a. Your, cousin Abe
   (b) Your cousin, Abe
3. a. We're ordering apples cheese, and pears.
   (b) We're ordering apples, cheese, and pears.
   c. We're ordering apples cheese and, pears.
4. a. I said "Mark, this is the address."
   b. I said, "Mark this is the address."
   (c) I said, "Mark, this is the address."

page 41

Answer Key

page 42

marks to correct the mistakes.

end marks and commas.
- Turn to page 5 if you need to review the marks.

Favorite Book

Thurs May 2 2013

Dear Mikhail and newspaper staff

I was glad to see you asked for e-mails about favorite books until now my favorite books were biographies novels and travel books. I just finished reading my first how-to book. What an interesting book?

the title is How to Canoe. the book was written by Dr Simonia Lakes. It includes text photos and drawings. Austin Tx is the hometown of dr Lakes She likes to canoe near Jones Ave in austin.

Have you ever read a book that made you want to run out and try something Well that's how I felt after I finished this book. I said "Grandma will you canoe with us" She said "Mya I would love to take you on a canoeing trip." We're going next week, and i can't wait!

Best Wishes

Mya

Mya

page 43

Favorite Book

Thurs., May 2, 2013

Dear Mikhail and Newspaper Staff,

I was glad to see you asked for e-mails about favorite books. Until now, my favorite books were biographies, novels, and travel books. I just finished reading my first how-to book. What an interesting book!

The title is How to Canoe. The book was written by Dr. Simonia Lakes. It includes text, photos, and drawings. Austin, TX is the hometown of Dr. Lakes. She likes to canoe near Jones Ave. in Austin.

Have you ever read a book that made you want to run out and try something? Well, that's how I felt after I finished this book. I said, "Grandma, will you canoe with us?" She said, "Mya, I would love to take you on a canoeing trip." We're going next week, and I can't wait!

Best wishes,

Mya

B. *Circle the correct answer choice.*

B. 1. a 2. c 3. c 4. a

page 44

... quotation marks. Use proofreading marks to correct the mistakes.

Dan asked, "When is the report due?"
- Use this mark to add a quotation mark.

Dan said, Let's go home."
- Use this mark to take away a quotation mark.

"Dan said, "Let's go home."

School Greeting Cards

by José Juarez

The sale of greeting cards will be coming up next month. Ms. Ayoub says This will be the biggest project for the spring. We hope everyone will help". Mr. Jonas says, "We need writers, artists, and students to make sales and pass out the cards

Students will write some of the cards. But some of the cards will be written by the senders. Donny Garza is in charge of the project. He says, "There will be a charge for writing and a separate charge for artwork".

I asked, How many cards were sent out last year? Donny explained that students sent almost 200 cards last year. "What a great year we had! he said.

A fifth grader told me, I hope we'll have even better sales this year"!

If you would like to sign up to help, go to the lunchroom after school on Thursday. Donny says We will be offering refreshments and fun, so be sure to come!

44 Oh Yeah? Proof It! Grade 4

page 45

School Greeting Cards by José Juarez

The sale of greeting cards will be coming up next month. Ms. Ayoub says, "This will be the biggest project for the spring. We hope everyone will help." Mr. Jonas says, "We need writers, artists, and students to make sales and pass out the cards."

Students will write some of the cards. But some of the cards will be written by the senders. Donny Garza is in charge of the project. He says, "There will be a charge for writing and a separate charge for artwork."

I asked, "How many cards were sent out last year?" Donny explained that students sent almost 200 cards last year. "What a great year we had!" he said.

A fifth grader told me, "I hope we'll have even better sales this year!"

If you would like to sign up to help, go to the lunchroom after school on Thursday. Donny says, "We will be offering refreshments and fun, so be sure to come!"

B. *Write a brief article to tell about a school event or classroom discussion.*
- The article may be fiction or nonfiction.
- Include at least three quotes.
- Show quotation end marks of at least one period, one question mark, and one exclamation mark.

Articles will vary, but should address a school event or classroom discussion. The article should be correctly punctuated and should include at least three quotes which each use one end mark: a period, a question mark, or an exclamation mark.

page 46

Steps to the Treasure

by Porfiria Ang

or play.

"On Our Way"
- Use quotation marks for the title of a poem.
  "Stopping by Woods on a Snowy Evening"
- Underline the title of a book.
  A Wrinkle in Time
- Use this mark to add underlining.
  A Wrinkle in Time
- Remember the marks for adding and taking away quotation marks. Turn to page 5 if you need to review the marks.

I just finished reading a new book titled Steps to the Treasure. It was written by Benjamin Gade. This was an excellent book. After I read the first chapter, Day One of the Treasure Hunt, I couldn't put the book down.

The characters were very strong in the book, and the plot was really unusual. The characters had many lessons to learn as they solved the story problem. This book reminded me of the book Gulliver's Travels. The characters had to travel to many lands as they looked for the treasure.

The characters sang as they traveled. This helped them from feeling scared. One of the songs they sang was Merrily, We Roll Along.

Our teacher asked us to write poems about the books we read. We put our poems on posters. The title of my poem was The Treasure at the End of the Rainbow.

You can see my posters and other students' posters in the main hall. You'll learn more about all of the interesting books we've been reading!

46 Oh Yeah? Proof It! Grade 4

page 47

A. *Correctly rewrite the book review.*

Steps to the Treasure

by Porfiria Ang

I just finished reading a new book titled Steps to the Treasure. It was written by Benjamin Gade. This was an excellent book. After I read the first chapter, "Day One of the Treasure Hunt," I couldn't put the book down.

The characters were very strong in the book, and the plot was really unusual. The characters had many lessons to learn as they solved the story problem. This book reminded me of the book Gulliver's Travels. The characters had to travel to many lands as they looked for the treasure.

The characters sang as they traveled. This helped them from feeling scared. One of the songs they sang was "Merrily, We Roll Along."

Our teacher asked us to write poems about the books we read. We put our poems on posters. The title of my poem was "The Treasure at the End of the Rainbow."

You can see my posters and other students' posters in the main hall. You'll learn more about all of the interesting books we've been reading!

B. *Correctly write the title of one of each of the following. Do not include any of the titles from the book review.*

1. One of your favorite songs:
3. One of your favorite poems:

1–4: Answers will vary, but should be correctly punctuated.

Answer Key

Chapter by Chapter

Chapter by Chapter is having A bookstore blowout sale! come to the finest bookstore in Town! We promise You won't be disappointed. We sell sheet music books magazines and Plays. Our manager is ms sullivan She says please let me know if you have any questions when you visit the store Our customers say "this is the best bookstore in the City. we will have a great time shopping there" or !

This is Our Address.
491 venus Rd
Aames Va

these are some of Our sale Books.
the Wizard Of Oz
Madge And Nan
Spiders flies And ants

What a good selection of plays we have?
a Country divided
Tiana And The whale
Eleanor Of Aquitane

You'll find these short Stories in our Magazines and Books
my Favorite aunt
the Work To Build again
Back On The basketball Court

48 Oh Yeah? Proof It! Grade 4

page 48

Chapter by Chapter

Chapter by Chapter is having a bookstore blowout sale! Come to the finest bookstore in town! (or .) We promise you won't be disappointed. We sell sheet music, books, magazines, and plays. Our manager is Ms. Sullivan. She says, "Please let me know if you have any questions when you visit the store." Our customers say, "This is the best bookstore in the city. We will have a great time shopping there. (or !)"

This is our address.
491 Venus Rd.
Aames, VA

These are some of our sale books.
The Wizard Of Oz
Madge and Nan
Spiders, Flies, and Ants

What a good selection of plays we have!
A Country Divided
Tiana and the Whale
Eleanor of Aquitane

You'll find these short stories in our magazines and books. (or !)
"My Favorite Aunt"
"The Work to Build Again"
"Back on the Basketball Court"

page 49

has made some mistakes with apostrophes. Use proofreading marks to correct the mistakes.

- Use this mark to add an apostrophe. don't
- Use this mark to take away an apostrophe. do'n't

will + not = won't

Possible Flooding

by Will Sanderson

Rain has been falling for a full week now. The river won't stop rising. We've tried putting sandbags around the lake. Everyone is hoping the sandbags will help to keep the town from flooding.

We haven't had a flood in our town since the 1950s. Most can't even imagine what it would be like. The town is carefully preparing.

You shouldn't be scared, though. There is a good chance the rain will stop soon, and the sandbags couldn't be stronger or set higher.

If the water doesn't stop rising tomorrow, school will be closed. We haven't ever had to do this, though. So, were thinking everything should be fine.

City officials can't say strongly enough that people shouldn't be worried at this point. We're all watching the news and the warnings. Next week, we hope we'll be able to print an article about the water level dropping.

50 Oh Yeah? Proof It! Grade 4

page 50

Possible Flooding

by Will Sanderson

Rain has been falling for a full week now. The river won't stop rising. We've tried putting sandbags around the lake. Everyone is hoping the sandbags will help to keep the town from flooding.

We haven't had a flood in our town since the 1950s. Most can't even imagine what it would be like. The town is carefully preparing.

You shouldn't be scared, though. There is a good chance the rain will stop soon, and the sandbags couldn't be stronger or set higher.

If the water doesn't stop rising tomorrow, school will be closed. We haven't ever had to do this, though. So, we're thinking everything should be fine.

City officials can't say strongly enough that people shouldn't be worried at this point. We're all watching the news and the warnings. Next week, we hope we'll be able to print an article about the water level dropping.

B. Circle the correct answer choice.

B. 1. a 2. c 3. a 4. b

page 51

Please! Help!

- For most plural nouns, add an apostrophe after the -s. dogs' dishes
- Remember the marks for adding and taking away apostrophes. Turn to page 5 if you need to review the marks.

Jims cats have disappeared. Their names are Kit and Kat. Kits fur is brown. Kats fur is black. Both cats collars are purple.

Note from Jim: My familys house is near the park. The cats dashed out our front door. All of our neighbors have been looking for the cats. Our neighbors cries, all of them, have gone unanswered. We think the cats are still somewhere in the park. Thank you for your help!

This is the flyer Jims dad has put up in Town Square. ---------------- Our cats are missing. They disappeared on Monday, May 9. We last saw them near the park's sandbox. Please call us if you see them. 123-456-7891

52 Oh Yeah? Proof It! Grade 4

page 52

Correctly rewrite the ad.

Please! Help!

Jim's cats have disappeared. Their names are Kit and Kat. Kit's fur is brown. Kat's fur is black. Both cats' collars are purple.

Note from Jim: My family's house is near the park. The cats dashed out our front door. All of our neighbors have been looking for the cats. Our neighbors' cries, all of them, have gone unanswered. We think the cats are still somewhere in the park. Thank you for your help!

This is the flyer Jim's dad has put up in Town Square. ---------------- Our cats are missing. They disappeared on Monday, May 9. We last saw them near the park's sandbox. Please call us if you see them. 123-456-7891

page 53

Answer Key

Underground Railroad

Aug 5 2013

Dear students

What an interesting trip we took last week we went to see an old house near our town. Long ago it was a hiding place. it was a station on the underground railroad. When i walked inside i was amazed It was as though i had stepped back in time.

The person in charge was ms daily She told us all about the underground railroad. She said Mary people were on their way to safety when they traveled."

I told my mother "You know mom this is better than any other trip we've taken. At the end of the tour we visited a shop at the front of the house. I bought a book titled "The way To Safety." My brother bought a poetry collection. his favorite poem in the collection is titled Waiting For Freedom and the books cover is beautiful.

Next year i hope well get to visit again Until then i hope to continue to learn more about the Underground railroad

Your Friend

Naisha

54 Oh Yeah? Proof It! Grade 4

page 54

Aug. 5, 2013

Dear Students,

What an interesting trip we took last week! We went to see an old house near our town. Long ago, it was a hiding place. It was a station on the Underground Railroad. When I walked inside, I was amazed! (or .) It was as though I had stepped back in time.

The person in charge was Ms. Daly. She told us all about the Underground Railroad. She said, "Many people were on their way to safety when they traveled."

I told my mother, "You know, Mom, this is better than any other trip we've taken. At the end of the tour, we visited a shop at the front of the house. I bought a book titled The Way to Safety. My brother bought a poetry collection. His favorite poem in the collection is titled "Waiting for Freedom," and the book's cover is beautiful.

Next year, I hope we'll get to visit again. (or !) Until then, I hope to continue to learn more about the Underground Railroad. (or !)

Your friend,

Naisha

page 55

- The words *me, him, her, us,* and *them* are direct objects.
  Throw the ball to me.
  I will throw it to you.
  She is in the lunchroom with him.
  He is at school with her.
  They are in the car with us.
- Use these marks to take away one word and add another.
  Him will give it to they.

Help the School Bake Sale! A Note from Tim Fields: Student Head of Sales

Us need help with the school bake sale. Mr. Wong is the sponsor. Him has been working hard to plan the sale. Ms. Chastain is also helping with the sale. Her and Mr. Wong will both be happy to answer questions or take your name on the sign-up sheet.

Mr. Wong and me have spent time planning. Us have been helped by many other students. You and me can work together with other students to set up the tables.

Speak to Mr. Wong or Ms. Chastain if you want to help they with next year's sale. Them will be happy to tell you about next year's plans.

56 Oh Yeah? Proof It! Grade 4

page 56

Help the School Bake Sale! A Note from Tim Fields: Student Head of Sales

We need help with the school bake sale. Mr. Wong is the sponsor. He has been working hard to plan the sale. Ms. Chastain is also helping with the sale. She and Mr. Wong will both be happy to answer questions or take your name on the sign-up sheet.

Mr. Wong and I have spent time planning. We have been helped by many other students. You and I can work together with other students to set up the tables.

Speak to Mr. Wong or Ms. Chastain if you want to help them with next year's sale. They will be happy to tell you about next year's plans.

page 57

Read the story. The writer has made some errors with double negatives. Use proofreading marks to take away incorrect words and add the correct words.

- A negative word is a word that has a meaning like *no* or *not*.
  no not never nowhere nobody nothing
- Do not use double negatives, two negative words together. This includes negative contractions, such as:
  can't won't doesn't hadn't shouldn't didn't couldn't wouldn't
- Remember the marks for adding and taking away words. Turn to page 5 if you need to review the marks.

No Movies for Me?

by Lana Michaels

My friends didn't not want (didn't want (or did not want)) to stay home all day. It was raining. There wasn't not (was not (or wasn't)) much to do. My friends asked if I wanted to go to the movies. I hadn't never (hadn't ever (or had never)) seen the movie they were going to see, so I agreed to go. I couldn't (could) hardly wait to meet my friends.

There's not nothing (nothing (or not anything)) better than going to the movies on a rainy day. The movie theater is not nowhere (nowhere (or not anywhere)) near our neighborhood, so a parent had to drive.

We got to the theater. I reached into my bag. Oh, no! I couldn't find my money nowhere (anywhere). The money wasn't nowhere (was nowhere (or wasn't anywhere)) to be found, and none of my friends didn't have (had) enough money to loan to me. I thought I'd have to call someone to come pick me up and take me home.

Then one of my friends asked if I'd checked in the pocket of my jeans. I couldn't not (couldn't (or could not)) believe it. But the money was way in the bottom of my pocket. I hadn't never (had never (or hadn't ever)) been so embarrassed. Everyone laughed, and we all enjoyed the movie. I didn't never (didn't ever (or did not ever)) want to go through that again. I won't never (won't ever (or will not ever or will never)) again forget to check for my money before I leave home.

58 Oh Yeah? Proof It! Grade 4

page 58

No Movies for Me?

by Lana Michaels

My friends didn't want (or did not want) to stay home all day. It was raining. There was not (or wasn't) much to do. My friends asked if I wanted to go to the movies. I hadn't ever (or had never) seen the movie they were going to see, so I agreed to go. I could hardly wait to meet my friends.

There's nothing (or not anything) better than going to the movies on a rainy day. The movie theater is nowhere (or not anywhere) near our neighborhood, so a parent had to drive.

We got to the theater. I reached into my bag. Oh, no! I couldn't find my money anywhere. The money was nowhere (or wasn't anywhere) to be found, and none of my friends had enough money to loan to me. I thought I'd have to call someone to come pick me up and take me home.

Then one of my friends asked if I'd checked in the pocket of my jeans. I couldn't (or could not) believe it. But the money was way in the bottom of my pocket. I had never (or hadn't ever) been so embarrassed. Everyone laughed, and we all enjoyed the movie. I didn't ever (or did not ever) want to go through that again. I won't ever (or will not ever or will never) again forget to check for my money before I leave home.

page 59

ANSWER KEY

has confused some words. Use proofreading marks to correct the writer's mistakes.

Book Donations

by Rick Pauls

A fire started in our town library last week. It burned the library to the ground. Your book donations are needed to help the library. The librarians say that they're needs include books of all kinds. They would like to receive magazines, to.

What will the future of the library bee? You can help two decide, and it won't cost you a sent. Just give old books you can spare.

"Were working around the clock," the head librarian told us. "You can bring your books hear to the grocery store. Its next door to the spot were the library used to be. Look for the store with the big green, read, and blew letters on the sign. Were collecting books back in the sail section."

Please give you're extra books. Everyone who donates will be a special guessed at a party when the library opens again. We don't know how many people will give. But we hope many will, sew the library can open again soon.

...meaning of these words. Here are some examples.

your you're
their they're there
its it's
to too two
were we're where
here hear
who's whose
be bee
blue blew
cent scent sent

60 Oh Yeah? Proof It! Grade 4

page 60

Book Donations by Rick Pauls

A fire started in our town library last week. It burned the library to the ground. Your book donations are needed to help the library. The librarians say that their needs include books of all kinds. They would like to receive magazines, too.

What will the future of the library be? You can help to decide, and it won't cost you a cent. Just give old books you can spare.

"We're working around the clock," the head librarian told us. "You can bring your books here to the grocery store. It's next door to the spot where the library used to be. Look for the store with the big green, red, and blue letters on the sign. We're collecting books back in the sale section."

Please give your extra books. Everyone who donates will be a special guest at a party when the library opens again. We don't know how many people will give. But we hope many will, so the library can open again soon.

B. *Follow directions to write sentences below.*

1. On a separate sheet of paper, write two sentences about your neighborhood. Correctly use one of the words below in each sentence.

   who's whose

   Answers will vary. Each of the two sentences should tell something about the community and correctly include one of these words: *who's, whose.*

2. On a separate sheet of paper, write three sentences about your state. Correctly use one of the words below in each sentence.

   were we're where

   Answers will vary. Each of the three sentences should tell something about the student's state and correctly include one of these words: *were, we're, where.*

page 61

The Life of a Teacher

by Susan Prof

We had an assignment to read two books. One was fiction. The other was nonfiction. The nonfiction book I read was The Life of a Teacher. It was definitely the best of the two books. The author writes very good.

The book helped me understand how the life of one teacher was hardest than the lives of many others. He was the favoritest teacher in his school. He worked the harder of all the teachers. He prepared even gooder work than he had the year before.

This was an excellent book. It told about the teacher, and it also told about the teacher's bestest friend. The friend was the happier of all the people the teacher knew. She helped the teacher learn how to do an even gooder job every day.

I think everyone should read this book. It is about the wiser people I have ever read about in a book. It will make you think about the work of teachers. It will also help you think about how to make your own life gooder.

- For most adjectives, add *-er* to compare two people, places, or things.
- For most adjectives, add *-est* to compare more than two people, places, or things.
- Use the word *good* to describe one person, place, or thing. Use the word *better* to describe two people places or things. Use the word *best* to describe three or more.

62 Oh Yeah? Proof It! Grade 4

page 62

The Life of a Teacher

by Susan Prof

We had an assignment to read two books. One was fiction. The other was nonfiction. The nonfiction book I read was The Life of a Teacher. It was definitely the better of the two books. The author writes very well.

The book helped me understand how the life of one teacher was harder than the lives of many others. He was the favorite teacher in his school. He worked the hardest of all the teachers. He prepared even better work than he had the year before.

This was an excellent book. It told about the teacher, and it also told about the teacher's best friend. The friend was the happiest of all the people the teacher knew. She helped the teacher learn how to do an even better job every day.

I think everyone should read this book. It is about the wisest people I have ever read about in a book. It will make you think about the work of teachers. It will also help you think about how to make your own life better.

B. *Circle the correct answer choice.*

B. 1. c 2. a 3. b 4. a

page 63

Skool Speakers for Next Year

Deer Keisha,

I wuz glad the newspaper askt for ideas for nekst year's speekers. I wud like to have more peepul kome in to talk abowt and show animulz. Last yeer, we bot some hamsters for our class. They did not kost too much. Wee bot them with the monee we recieved from the bake sale. We have allreddy lurned so much abowt these animulz, and they are so kute.

I know everywon is really bizzy, but it wud be nice to arrange for snakes, spidurs, and other creatures to be shown to students. I have hurd that a groop in town goze to classes to show them.

I wud be hapy to save my pennys from change to giv to a fund to bring in these creturez. Neither of the fourth grade classes has seen these presentations. They wud be realy speshul. Becuz we want this so much, we hope it wil be posible.

It is quiet intereseting to lurn about new things. Some peepul thingk these critters are feirce, but I don't agre. I loook forwurd to reeding about othur students' ideas.

Sincerly,

Diana

Diana

64 Oh Yeah? Proof It! Grade 4

page 64

School Speakers for Next Year

Dear Keisha,

I was glad the newspaper asked for ideas for next year's speakers. I would like to have more people come in to talk about and show animals. Last year, we bought some hamsters for our class. They did not cost too much. We bought them with the money we received from the bake sale. We have already learned so much about these animals, and they are so cute.

I know everyone is really busy, but it would be nice to arrange for snakes, spiders, and other creatures to be shown to students. I have heard that a group in town goes to classes to show them.

I would be happy to save my pennies from change to give to a fund to bring in these creatures. Neither of the fourth grade classes has seen these presentations. They would be really special. Because we want this so much, we hope it will be possible.

It is quite interesting to learn about new things. Some people think these critters are fierce, but I don't agree. I look forward to reading about other students' ideas.

Sincerely,

Diana

B. *Circle the answer choice in which all words are spelled correctly.*

B. 1. c 2. a 3. c 4. b

page 65

Answer Key

Garden Shop

Kome to our huje sale. You will not be disapointed. One of our kustomerz sez, "You culdn't finde a bedder deal anywere! It wud be a terribul shame to mis this sale!"

Wee hav flowerz for partys and all speshul events. Wee evun have a cuboard filled with tiny flowerz for hollidays.

Do you wunt to take sumthing to ur teehur? We hav wut you need!

How doese our stor ofer such gud priceing? We groe the flowerz here! You kan walk throug our stor and see the garduns in the back of the bilding. Be our gest!

66 Oh Yeah? Proof It! Grade 4

page 66

Garden Shop

Come to our huge sale. You will not be disappointed. One of our customers says, "You couldn't find a better deal anywhere! It would be a terrible shame to miss this sale!"

We have flowers for parties and all special events. We even have a cupboard filled with tiny flowers for holidays.

Do you want to take something to your teacher? We have what you need!

How does our store offer such good pricing? We grow the flowers here! You can walk through our store and see the gardens in the back of the building. Be our guest!

page 67

...negatives, comparison, and spelling. Use proofreading marks to correct the writer's mistakes.

Remember... proofreading marks you have learned. Turn to page 5 if you need to review the marks.

Charles Lindbergh

by Ralph Voler

My freind and me went to the libray. I red a very gud article. It was one of the most goodest articles I have ever red. I hasn't never been so intrested in an article.

The article wuz abowt Charles Lindbergh. Flyeeng acrost the oshun in an airplain mite not seem unushual today. But that wuz not the case wen Lindbergh wuz in the air.

In 1927, Lindbergh flew akros the see. He landed in Paris. Nobody had never done this befour.

Lindbergh beleived that plains flying akrost an oshun wud bekum a vury importunt part uv transportashun. You no whut? He wuz write!

Twoday, plains fly to many countrys. They cary peepul. They cary items that hav bin sold. They delivur things that have bin cent to you and i.

Won day, I hope well be abul to fly up hi in a plain. Untill then, we kan dreem abowt it.

68 Oh Yeah? Proof It! Grade 4

page 68

Charles Lindbergh

by Ralph Voler

My friend and I went to the library. I read a very good article. It was one of the best articles I have ever read. I haven't ever (or have never) been so interested in an article.

The article was about Charles Lindbergh. Flying across the ocean in an airplane might not seem unusual today. But that was not the case when Lindbergh was in the air.

In 1927, Lindbergh flew across the sea. He landed in Paris. Nobody had ever done this before.

Lindbergh believed that planes flying across an ocean would become a very important part of transportation. You know what? He was right!

Today, planes fly to many countries. They carry people. They carry items that have been sold. They deliver things that have been sent to you and me.

One day, I hope we'll be able to fly up high in a plane. Until then, we can dream about it.

page 69

The Windy City

FRID Apr 2

To Michelle and the other editors,

I am happy you asked stoodents to rite about one of there most favoritest citys. One of mine is chicago. you know my Mom and me visited this city last year. She said this is a realy beeutiful place! I haven't never been nowhere so lovely.

do you no wat i lurnt abowt chicago. It is also known as the Windy City. Why is this. Sum thingk its beeuz their is sew much wind in the city. Its true that there is plenty uv wind. But this is knot the reezun for the name.

Long ago peepul told long tails about how wunderful the city wuz. They wanted chicago to be choosen as the place for the 1893 world's Fair. They sed so many theengs and spoke so much and fur such a long time that the citie got it's niknamе. It wuz sed two bee windy beeuz of peepul talking and talking abowt the citie! i am glad i cud share this infurmashun with you.

A Chicago Fan

Monique

70 Oh Yeah? Proof It! Grade 4

page 70

Fri., (or Friday) Apr. 2

To Michelle and the Other Editors,

I am happy you asked students to write about one of their favorite cities. One of mine is Chicago. You know, my mom and I visited this city last year. She said, "This is a really beautiful place! I haven't ever (or have never) been anywhere so lovely."

Do you know what I learned about Chicago? It is also known as the Windy City. Why is this? Some think it's because there is so much wind in the city. It's true that there is plenty of wind. But this is not the reason for the name.

Long ago, people told long tales about how wonderful the city was. They wanted Chicago to be chosen as the place for the 1893 World's Fair. They said so many things and spoke so much and for such a long time that the city got its nickname. It was said to be windy because of people talking and talking about the city! I am glad I could share this information with you.

A Chicago fan,

Monique

page 71

Read the story. The writer made some mistakes with sentences. Use proofreading marks to correct the mistakes.

Chugging Along

by Nan Trak

"All aboard!" the conductor yells. He is wearing a blue suit. Tina steps on board the train. It is her first train ride. She finds an empty seat. Then she settles in for the long ride.

Tina is nervous. She sits near a window. Tina looks out at the countryside.

Soon, Tina sees farms and forests race by. The colors all blend together. Tina is less nervous now. She looks at the other people on the train. They don't look nervous. Some are reading. Some are talking.

The train ride finally ends. Tina steps carefully off of the train. She sees her grandmother. The two hug. Then they leave the train station. Tina knows this is going to be a wonderful vacation.

Remember — Sentences

- A sentence tells a complete thought. It includes a complete subject and a complete predicate.
  Sentence: The colorful fall leaves swirled to the ground.
- A fragment does not tell a complete thought. It does not include a complete subject and a complete predicate.
  Fragment: The colorful fall leaves.
  Fragment: Swirled to the ground.
  The colorful fall leaves swirled to the ground.
- A run-on tells more than one complete thought. It must be broken into individual sentences.
  Run-on: The colorful fall leaves swirl to the ground they are lovely to watch.
  The colorful fall leaves swirl to the ground. They are lovely to watch.
- Remember that a verb must agree with its subject.
  The teacher is in the lunchroom.
  Teachers are in the lunchroom.

72 Oh Yeah? Proof It! Grade 4

page 72

Chugging Along

by Nan Trak

"All aboard!" the conductor yells. He is wearing a blue suit. Tina steps on board the train. It is her first train ride. She finds an empty seat. Then she settles in for the long ride.

Tina is nervous. She sits near a window. Tina looks out at the countryside.

Soon, Tina sees farms and forests race by. The colors all blend together. Tina is less nervous now. She looks at the other people on the train. They don't look nervous. Some are reading. Some are talking.

The train ride finally ends. Tina steps carefully off of the train. She sees her grandmother. The two hug. Then they leave the train station. Tina knows this is going to be a wonderful vacation.

B. *Circle the answer choice that is a complete sentence.*

B. 1. a 2. c 3. b 4. a

page 73

Use this mark to show where a new paragraph should begin. ¶

It is important to write sentences that flow. Sometimes, it is necessary to combine sentences to improve the flow of a paragraph.
The storm brought rain. The storm brought wind. The storm brought lightning.
The storm brought rain, wind, and lightning.

... has written the whole article as one long paragraph, and many of the sentences are short and choppy. Use proofreading marks to combine sentences and to show where each new paragraph should start.

Author Speaks to Students

by Bill Cramer

Author Keith Bhagwat came to speak to students last Wednesday. The author is also a chef. He wrote a book about his favorite recipes. The book explains how he learned to be a chef where he learned to be a chef and why he decided to learn to be a chef. ¶ First, Mr. Bhagwat discussed his childhood. His dad was a chef. His mom was a chef. His uncle was a chef. So, he was around cooking from the time he was very young. ¶ Next, Mr. Bhagwat told us about the kinds of dishes he enjoys cooking. He enjoys cooking with vegetables, spices, and noodles. He has enjoyed cooking with these ingredients for a long time. ¶ Finally, Mr. Bhagwat let us taste one of his most famous dishes. It was delicious! Everyone was very happy to have a sample. ¶ After Mr. Bhagwat finished speaking, he autographed copies of one of his recipes for us. We all hope he'll come back to our school again soon.

74 Oh Yeah? Proof It! Grade 4

page 74

Author Speaks to Students

by Bill Cramer

Author Keith Bhagwat came to speak to students last Wednesday. The author is also a chef. He wrote a book about his favorite recipes. The book explains how he learned to be a chef, where he learned to be a chef, and why he decided to learn to be a chef.

First, Mr. Bhagwat discussed his childhood. His dad was a chef. His mom was a chef. His uncle was a chef. So, he was around cooking from the time he was very young.

Next, Mr. Bhagwat told us about the kinds of dishes he enjoys cooking. He enjoys cooking with vegetables, spices, and noodles. He has enjoyed cooking with these ingredients for a long time.

Finally, Mr. Bhagwat let us taste one of his most famous dishes. It was delicious! Everyone was very happy to have a sample.

After Mr. Bhagwat finished speaking, he autographed copies of one of his recipes for us. We all hope he'll come back to our school again soon.

B. *Explain how you decided where it was necessary to start new paragraphs.*

Answers will vary but should include something about using the words *first, next,* and *finally.*

page 75

A Wrinkle in Time

by Cheena Amra

Remember the proofreading marks you have learned. Turn to page 5 if you need to review the marks.

In this book, a sister and brother travel through time and space. They know they must save their father. It was nice that the author let the children solve the problems in the book. Their action really makes you want to read more.

This is a good example of science fiction. It pulls in the reader's interest from the first moment. I won't give away the meaning of the title of the book, but I say, "Friends, you should read this book." What an ending! After reading, you'll be able to understand the title. You might even want to write science fiction for your next assignment.

Mr. Danel recommended A Wrinkle in Time to me, and I strongly recommend it to you. It is one of the finest books I have ever read. This book was written by Madeleine L'Engle. She writes descriptions that make you feel as though you are traveling through time right along with the characters.

You should read this book. It's excellent!

76 Oh Yeah? Proof It! Grade 4

page 76

A Wrinkle in Time

by Cheena Amra

In this book, a sister and brother travel through time and space. They know they must save their father. It was nice that the author let the children solve the problems in the book. Their action really makes you want to read more.

This is a good example of science fiction. It pulls in the reader's interest from the first moment. I won't give away the meaning of the title of the book. But I say, "Friends, you should read this book." What an ending! After reading, you'll be able to understand the title. You might even want to write science fiction for your next assignment.

Mr. Danel recommended A Wrinkle in Time to me, and I strongly recommend it to you. It is one of the finest books I have ever read. This book was written by Madeleine L'Engle. She writes descriptions that make you feel as though you are traveling through time right along with the characters.

You should read this book. It's excellent!

page 77

Answer Key

What a Visit!

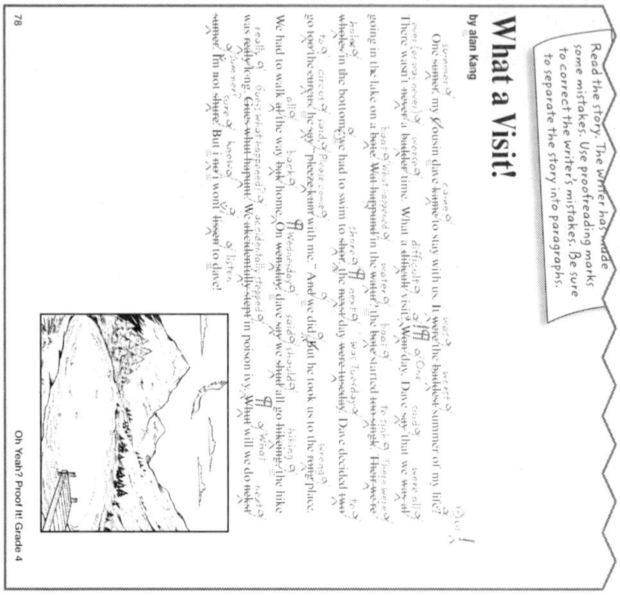

page 78

page 79

page 80

That's Already Lost!

page 81

Art Show

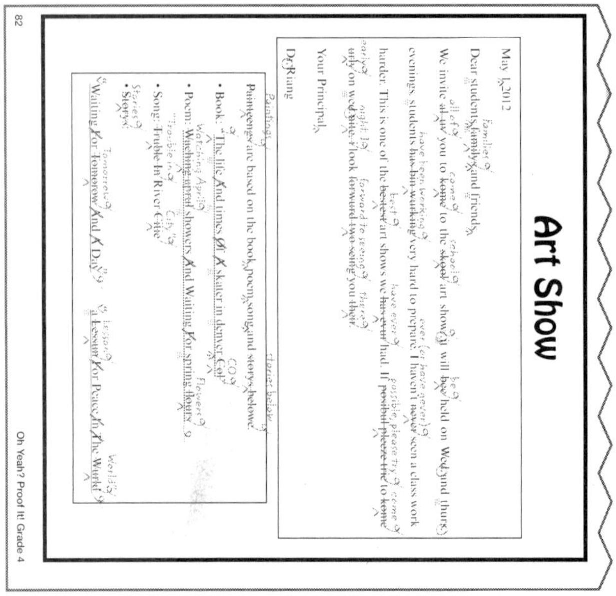

page 82

Art Show

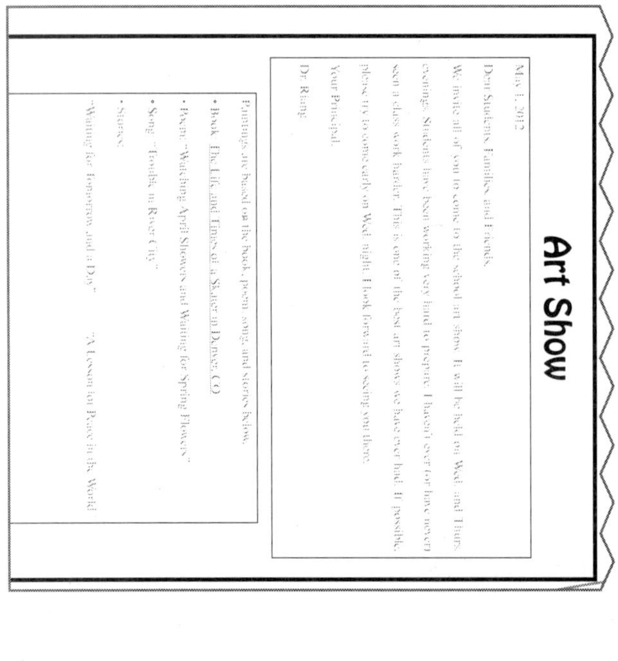

page 83